Erckmann-Chatrian

The Conscript

a story of the French war of 1813

Erckmann-Chatrian

The Conscript
a story of the French war of 1813

ISBN/EAN: 9783337844769

Printed in Europe, USA, Canada, Australia, Japan

Cover: Foto ©ninafisch / pixelio.de

More available books at **www.hansebooks.com**

THE CONSCRIPT:

A STORY

OF

THE FRENCH WAR OF 1813.

BY

MM. ERCKMANN-CHATRIAN.

TRANSLATED FROM THE TWENTIETH PARIS EDITION.

With Eight full page Illustrations.

———

NEW YORK:
CHARLES SCRIBNER AND COMPANY.
1870.

Entered, according to Act of Congress, in the year 1868,
By CHARLES SCRIBNER AND COMPANY,
In the Clerk's office of the District Court of the United States for the Southern District of New York.

ADVERTISEMENT.

THE following extract from the preface to the illustrated edition of the Erckmann-Chatrian novels recently published in Paris, will give American readers an idea of the high place which these works hold in French Literature. The editors of the series write:

"Never has pen been held by a firmer and honester hand than that which has traced the admirable, glorious, thrilling stories which unfold themselves in the books we bring together under the name of '*National Novels.*' Never has our history been approached with greater directness and honesty than in these works, at once so thrilling and so simple. Not a word in these ingenuous and profound tales can wound the conscience of the citizen or alarm the modesty of the fireside. In these books there is moral food which one can offer without apprehension to the whole family circle; father, mother, children, grandfather may read them together, and after having read them all, yes—all, we are warranted in saying—will feel that they are better and stronger. Each of these works is the representation of one of the great wars of the Revolution, and of the Empire. Our fathers have preserved and handed down to us the memory of these great struggles which formerly shook France from centre to circumference, which survive to-day in the recollection of many still living:—the old soldier, the peasant, the laborer, will review with emotion and pride, in the 'National Novels,' the faithful record of the times which tried and tested them. There is in these admirable stories a severe simplicity which adapts them at once to readers of every age, and of all tastes.

"We cannot doubt that every one will co-operate according to his ability, in circulating these excellent works; we appeal to all patriotic hearts, to all fair minds which understand that if bad books are to be feared, the antidote can only be found in reading sound, healthful works,—and that the 'National Novels' deserve to be classed among these, is the universal verdict."

LIST OF ILLUSTRATIONS.

		PAGE
I.—Monsieur Goulden,		*Frontispiece*
II.—"Come, my Children; to Table!"		38
III.—"Qui Vive?"		74
IV.—"Look Yonder,"		108
V.—"There are kind People in the World,"		120
VI.—"What makes you cry so, Josephel?"		219
VII.—"A dozen Bullets whistled through the Branches,"		274
VIII.—"I awoke in a Good Bed,"		324

THE STORY OF A CONSCRIPT.

I.

Those who have not seen the glory of the Emperor Napoleon, during the years 1810, 1811, and 1812, can never conceive what a pitch of power one man may reach.

When he passed through Champagne, or Lorraine, or Alsace, people gathering the harvest or the vintage would leave everything to run and see him; women, children, and old men would come a distance of eight or ten leagues to line his route, and cheer and cry, "*Vive l'Empereur! Vive l'Empereur!*" One would think that he was a god, that mankind owed its life to him, and that, if he died, the world would crumble and be no more. A few old Republicans would shake their heads and mutter over their wine that the Emperor might yet fall, but they passed for fools. Such an event appeared contrary to nature, and no one even gave it a thought.

I was in my apprenticeship since 1804, with an old watchmaker, Melchior Goulden, at Phalsbourg. As I seemed weak and was a little lame, my mother wished me to learn an easier trade than those of our village, for at Dagsberg there were only wood-cutters and charcoal-burners. Monsieur Goulden liked me very much. We lived on the first story of a large house opposite the "Red Ox" inn, and near the French gate.

That was the place to see princes, ambassadors, and generals come and go, some on horseback and some in carriages drawn by two or four horses; there they passed in embroidered uniforms, with waving plumes and decorations, from every country under the sun. And in the highway what couriers, what baggage-wagons, what powder-trains, cannon, caissons, cavalry, and infantry did we see! Those were stirring times!

In five or six years the innkeeper, George, had made a fortune. He had fields, orchards, houses, and money in abundance; for all these people, coming from Germany, Switzerland, Russia, Poland, or elsewhere, cared little for a few handfuls of gold scattered upon their road; they were all nobles, who took a pride in showing their prodigality.

From morning until night, and even during the night, the "Red Ox" kept its tables in readiness. Through the long windows on the first story nothing was to be seen but great white table-cloths, glittering with silver and covered with game, fish, and other rare viands, around which the travellers sat side by side. In the yard behind, horses neighed, postilions shouted, maid-servants laughed, coaches rattled. Ah! the hotel of the "Red Ox" will never see such prosperous times again.

Sometimes, too, people of the city stopped there, who in other times were known to gather sticks in the forest or to work on the highway. But now they were commandants, colonels, generals, and had won their grades by fighting in every land on earth.

Old Melchior, with his black silk cap pulled over his ears, his weak eyelids, his nose pinched between great horn spectacles, and his lips tightly pressed together, could not sometimes avoid putting aside his magnifying-glass and punch upon the work-bench, and throwing a glance toward the inn, especially when the cracking of the whips of the postilions, with their heavy boots, little jackets, and perukes of twisted hemp, awoke the the echoes of the ramparts and announced a new arrival. Then he became all attention, and from time to time would exclaim:

"Hold! It is the son of Jacob, the slater," or of "the old scold, Mary Ann," or of "the cooper, Frantz Sépel! He has made his way in the world; there he is, colonel and baron of the empire into the bargain. Why don't he stop at the house of his father, who lives yonder in the *Rue des Capucins?*"

But when he saw them shaking hands right and left in the street with those who recognized them, his tone changed; he wiped his eyes with his great spotted handkerchief, and murmured:

"How pleased poor old Annette will be! Good! good! *He* is not proud; he is a man. God preserve him from cannon-balls!"

Others passed as if ashamed to recognize their birth-place; others went gayly to see their sisters or cousins, and everybody spoke of them. One would imagine that all Phalsbourg wore their crosses and their epaulettes; while the arrogant were despised even more than when they swept the roads.

Nearly every month *Te Deums* were chanted, and the cannon at the arsenal fired their salutes of twenty-one rounds for some new victory, making one's heart flutter. During the week following every family was uneasy; poor mothers especially waited for letters, and the first that came all the city knew of; "such an one had received a letter from Jacques or Claude," and all ran to see if it spoke of their Joseph or their Jean-Baptiste. I do not speak of promotions or the official reports of deaths; as for the first, every one knew that the killed must be replaced; and as for the reports of deaths, parents awaited them weeping, for they did not come immediately; sometimes indeed they never came, and the poor father and mother hoped on, saying, "Perhaps our boy is a prisoner. When they make peace he will return. How many have returned whom we thought dead!"

But they never made peace. When one war was finished, another was begun. We always needed something, either from Russia or from Spain, or some other country. The Emperor was never satisfied.

married; but, if I should be so unfortunate as to be drawn in the conscription, there was an end of matters. I wished that I was a thousand times more lame; for at the time of which I speak they had first taken the unmarried men, then the married men who had no children, then those with one child; and I constantly asked myself, "Are lame fellows of more consequence than fathers of families? Could they not put me in the cavalry?" The idea made me so unhappy that I already thought of fleeing.

But in 1812, at the beginning of the Russian war, my fear increased. From February until the end of May, every day we saw pass regiments after regiments—dragoons, cuirassiers, carbineers, hussars, lancers of all colors, artillery, caissons, ambulances, wagons, provisions, rolling on forever, like a river which runs on and on, and of which one can never see the end.

I still remember that this began with soldiers driving large wagons drawn by oxen. These oxen were in the place of horses, and were to be used for food later on, when they should have used up their provisions. Everybody said, "What a fine idea!" When the soldiers can no longer feed the oxen, the oxen will feed the soldiers." Unhappily those who said this did not know that the oxen could only make seven or eight leagues a day, and that for every eight days of marching, they must have at least one day's rest; so that indeed, the poor animals' hoofs were already dry and worn out, their lips drooping, their eyes standing out of their heads, and little but skin and bone left of them. For three weeks they kept passing in this way, all torn with thrusts of the bayonet. Meat became cheap, for they killed many of the oxen; but few wanted their flesh, the diseased meat being unhealthy. They never went more than twenty leagues beyond the Rhine.

After that, we saw more lancers, sabres, and helmets file past. All flowed through the French gate, crossed the Place d'Armes, and streamed out at the German gate.

At last, on the 10th of May, in the year 1812, in the early morning, the guns of the arsenal announced the coming of the master of all. I was yet sleeping when the first shot shook the little panes of my window till they rattled like a drum, and Monsieur Goulden, with a lighted candle, opened my door, saying; "Get up, he is here!"

We opened the window. Through the night I saw a hundred dragoons, of whom many bore torches, enter at a gallop under the French gate; they shook the earth as they passed; their lights glanced along the house-fronts like dancing flames, and from every window we heard ceaseless shouts of "*Vive l'Empereur!*"

I was gazing at the carriage, when a horse crashed against the post to which the butcher Klein was accustomed to fasten his cattle. The dragoon fell heavily, his helmet rolled in the gutter, and immediately a head leaned out of the carriage to see what had happened—a large head, pale and fat, with a tuft of hair on the forehead: it was Napoleon; he held his hand up as if about taking a pinch of snuff, and said a few words roughly. The officer galloping by the side of the coach bent down to reply; and his master took his snuff and turned the corner, while the shouts redoubled and the cannons roared louder than ever.

This was all that I saw.

The Emperor did not stop at Phalsbourg, and, when he was on the road to Saverne, the guns fired their last shot, and silence reigned once more. The guards at the French gate raised the drawbridge, and the old watchmaker said:

"You have seen him?"

"I have, Monsieur Goulden."

"Well," he continued, "that man holds all our lives in his hand; he need but breathe upon us and we are gone. Let us bless Heaven that he is not evil-minded; for if he were, the world would see again the horrors of the days of the barbarian kings and the Turks."

He seemed lost in thought, but in a moment he added:

"You can go to bed again. The clock is striking three."

He returned to his room, and I to my bed. The deep silence without seemed strange after such a tumult, and until daybreak I never ceased dreaming of the Emperor. I dreamed, too, of the dragoon, and wanted to know if he were killed. The next day we learned that he was carried to the hospital and would recover.

From that day until the month of September they often sang the *Te Deum*, and fired twenty-one guns for new victories. It was nearly always in the morning, and Monsieur Goulden cried:

"Eh, Joseph! Another battle won! Fifty thousand men lost! Twenty-five standards, a hundred guns won. All goes well, all goes well. It only remains now to order a new levy to replace the dead!"

He pushed open my door, and I saw him, bald, in his shirt-sleeves, with his neck bare, washing his face in the wash-bowl.

"Do you think, Monsieur Goulden," I asked, in great trouble, "that they will also take the lame?"

"No, no," he said kindly; "fear nothing, my child, you could not serve. We will fix that. Only work well, and never mind the rest."

He saw my anxiety, and it pained him. I never met a better man. Then he dressed himself to go to wind up the city clocks—those of Monsieur the Commandant of the place, of Monsieur the Mayor, and other notable personages. I remained at home. Monsieur Goulden did not return until after the *Te Deum*. He took off his great brown coat, put his peruke back in its box, and again pulling his silk cap over his ears, said:

"The army is at Wilna or at Smolensk, as I learn from Monsieur the Commandant. God grant that we may succeed this time and make peace, and the sooner the better, for war is a terrible thing."

I thought, too, that, if we had peace, so many men would not be needed, and that I could marry Catharine. Any one can imagine the wishes I formed for the Emperor's glory.

II.

It was on the 15th of September, 1812, that the news came of the great victory of the Moskowa. Every one was full of joy, and all cried, "Now we will have peace! now the war is ended!"

Some discontented folks might say that China yet remained to be conquered; such mar-joys are always to be found.

A week after, we learned that our forces were in Moscow, the largest and richest city in Russia, and then everybody figured to himself the booty we would capture, and the reduction it would make in the taxes. But soon came the rumor that the Russians had set fire to their capital, and that it was necessary to retreat on Poland or to die of hunger. Nothing else was spoken of in the inns, the breweries, or the market; no one could meet his neighbor without saying. "Well, well, things go badly; the retreat has commenced."

People grew pale, and hundreds of peasants waited morning and night at the post-office, but no letters came now. I passed and repassed through the crowd without paying much attention to it, for I had seen so much of the same thing. And besides, I had a thought in my mind which gladdened my heart, and made everything seem rosy to me.

You must know that for six months past I had wished to make Catharine a magnificent present for her birth-day, which fell on the 18th of December. Among the watches which hung in Monsieur Goulden's window was one little one, of the prettiest kind, with a silver case full of little circles, which made it shine like a star. Around the face, under the glass, was a thread of copper, and on the face were painted two lovers, the youth evidently declaring his love, and giving to his sweetheart a large bouquet of roses, while she modestly lowered her eyes and held out her hand.

The first time I saw the watch, I said to myself; "You will not let that escape; that watch is for Catharine, and, although you must work every day till midnight for it, she must have it." Monsieur Goulden, after seven in the evening, allowed me work on my own account. He had old watches to clean and regulate; and as this work was often very troublesome, old Father Melchior paid me reasonably for it. But the little watch was thirty-five francs, and one can imagine how many hours at night I would have to work for it. I am sure that if Monsieur Goulden knew that I wanted it he would have given it me for a present, but I would not have let him take a farthing less for it; I would have regarded doing so something shameful. I kept saying: "You must earn it; no one else must have any claim upon it." Only for fear somebody else might take a fancy to buy it, I put it aside in a box, telling Father Melchior that I knew a purchaser.

Under these circumstances, every one can readily understand how it was that all these stories of war went in at one ear and out at the other with me. While I worked I imagined Catharine's joy, and for five months that was all I had before my eyes. I thought how pleased she would look, and asked myself, "What will she say?" Sometimes I imagined she would cry out, "Oh Joseph? what are you thinking of? It is much too beautiful for me. No, no; I cannot take so fine a watch from you!" Then I thought I would force it upon her; I would slip it into her apron-pocket, saying, "Come, come, Catharine! Do you wish to give me pain?" I could see how she wanted it, and that she spoke so only to seem to refuse it. Then I imagined her blushing, with her hands raised, saying, "Joseph, now I know indeed that you love me!" And she would embrace me with tears in her eyes. I felt very happy. Aunt Grédel approved of all. In a word, a thousand such scenes passed through my mind, and when I retired at night I thought: "There is no one as happy as you, Joseph. See what a present you can make Catharine by your toil; and she surely is preparing something for your birthday, for she thinks only of you; you are both very happy, and, when you are married, all will go well."

While I was thus working on, thinking only of happiness, the winter began, earlier than usual, toward the commencement of November. It did not begin with snow, but with dry, cold weather and heavy frosts. In a few days all the leaves had fallen and the earth was hard as ice and all covered with hoar-frost ; tiles, pavement, and window-panes glittered with it. Fires had to be made that winter to keep the cold from coming in at the windows, and, when the doors were opened for a moment, the heat seemed to disappear at once. The wood crackled in the stoves and burnt away like straw in the fierce draught of the chimneys.

Every morning I hastened to wash the panes of the shop-window with warm water, and I scarcely closed it when a frosty sheen covered it. Without, people ran puffing with their coat-collars over their ears and their hands in their pockets. No one stood still, and when doors opened, they soon closed.

I don't know what became of the sparrows, whether they were dead or living, but not one twittered in the chimneys, and save the reveille and retreat sounded in the barracks, no noise broke the silence.

Often when the fire crackled merrily, did Monsieur Goulden stop his work, and, gazing on the frost-covered panes, exclaim:

"Our poor soldiers! our poor soldiers!"

He said this so mournfully that I felt a choking in my throat as I replied:

"But, Monsieur Goulden, they ought now to be in Poland in good barracks; for to suppose that human beings could endure a cold like this— it is impossible."

"Such a cold as this," he said; "yes, here it is cold, very cold from the winds from the mountains; but what is this frost to that of the north, of Russia and of Poland? God grant that they started early enough. My God! my God! the leaders of men have a heavy weight to bear."

Then he would be silent, and for hours I would think of what he had said to me; I pictured to myself our soldiers on the march, running to keep themselves warm. But the thought of Catharine always came back to me, and I have often thought since that when one is happy, the misery of others affects him but little, especially in youth, when the passions are strongest, and when we have had little knowledge of great griefs.

After the frosts so much snow fell that the couriers were stopped on the road toward Quatre-Vents. I feared that I could not go to see Catharine on her fête-day; but two companies of infantry set out with pick-axes, and dug through the frozen snow a way for carriages, and that road remained open until the beginning of April, 1813.

Nevertheless, Catharine's birthday approached day by day, and my happiness increased in proportion. I had already the thirty-five francs, but I did not know how to tell Monsieur Goulden that I wished to buy the watch; I wanted to keep the whole matter secret; and I did not at all like to talk about it.

At length, on the eve of the eventful day, between six and seven in the evening, while we were working in silence, the lamp between us, suddenly I took my resolution, and said:

"You know, Monsieur Goulden, that I spoke to you of a purchaser for the little silver watch."

"Yes, Joseph," said he, without raising his head, "but he has not come yet."

"It is I who am the purchaser, Monsieur Goulden."

Then he looked up in astonishment. I took out the thirty-five francs and laid them on the work-bench. He stared at me.

"But," he said, "it is not such a watch as that you want, Joseph; you want one that will fill your pocket and mark the seconds. Those little watches are only for women."

I knew not what to say.

Monsieur Goulden, after meditating a few moments, began to smile.

"Ah!" he exclaimed; "good! good! I understand now; to-morrow is Catharine's birthday. Now I know why you worked day and night. Hold! take back this money; I do not want it."

I was all confusion.

"Monsieur Goulden, I thank you," I replied; "but this watch is for Catharine, and I wish to have earned it. You will pain me if you refuse the money; I would as lief not take the watch."

He said nothing more, but took the thirty-five francs; then he opened his drawer, and chose a pretty steel chain, with two little keys of silver-gilt, which he fastened to the watch. Then he put all together in a box with a rose-colored favor. He did all this slowly, as if affected; then he gave me the box.

"It is a pretty present, Joseph," said he. "Catharine ought to think herself happy in having such a lover as you. She is a good girl. Now we can take our supper. Set the table."

The table was arranged, and then Monsieur Goulden took from a closet a bottle of his Metz wine, which he kept for great occasions, and we supped like old friends, rather than as master and apprentice; all the evening he never stopped speaking of the merry days of his youth; telling me how he once had a sweetheart, but that, in 1792, he left home in the *levée en masse* at the time of the Prussian invasion, and that on his return to Fénétrange, he found her married—a very natural thing, since he had never mustered courage enough to declare his love. However, this did not prevent his remaining faithful to the tender remembrance, and when he spoke of it he seemed sad indeed. I recounted all this in imagination to Catharine, and it was not until the stroke of ten, at the passage of the rounds, which relieved the sentries on post every twenty minutes on account of the great cold, that we put two good logs on the fire, and at length went to bed.

III.

THE next day, the 18th of December, I arose about six in the morning. It was terribly cold; my little window was covered with a sheet of frost.

I had taken care the night before to lay out on the back of a chair my sky-blue coat, my trousers, my goat-skin vest, and my fine black silk cravat. Everything was ready; my well-polished shoes lay at the foot of the bed; I had only to dress myself; but the cold I felt upon my face, the sight of those window-panes, and the deep silence without, made me shiver in anticipation. If it had not been Catharine's birthday, I would have remained in bed until midday; but suddenly that recollection made me jump out of bed, and rush to the great delf stove, where some embers of the preceding night almost always remained among the cinders. I found two or three, and hastened to collect and put them under some split wood and two large logs, after which I ran back to my bed.

Monsieur Goulden, under the huge curtains, with the coverings pulled up to his nose and his cotton night-cap over his eyes, woke up, and cried out:

"Joseph, we have not had such cold for forty years. I never felt it so. What a winter we shall have!"

I did not answer, but looked out to see if the fire was lighting; the embers burnt well; I heard the chimney draw, and at once all blazed up. The sound of the flames was merry enough, but it required a good half-hour to feel the air any warmer.

At last I arose and dressed myself. Monsieur Goulden kept on chatting, but I thought only of Catharine, and when at length, toward eight o'clock, I started out, he exclaimed:

"Joseph, what are you thinking of? Are you going to Quatre-Vents in that little coat? You would be dead before you had got half way. Go into my closet, and take my great cloak, and the mittens, and the double-soled shoes lined with flannel."

I was so smart in my fine clothes that I reflected whether it would be better to follow his advice, and he, seeing my hesitation, said:

"Listen! a man was found frozen yesterday on the way to Wecham. Doctor Steinbrenner said that he sounded like a piece of dry wood when they tapped upon him. He was a soldier, and had left the village between six and seven o'clock, and at eight they found him; so that the frost did not take long to do its work. If you want your nose and ears frozen, you have only to go out as you are."

I knew then, that he was right; so I put on the thick shoes, and passed the cord of the mittens over my shoulders, and put the cloak over all. Thus accoutred, I sallied forth, after thanking Monsieur Goulden, who warned me not to stay too late, for the cold increased toward night, and great numbers of wolves were crossing the Rhine on the ice.

I had not gone as far as the church when I turned up the fox-skin collar of the cloak to shield my ears. The cold was so keen that it seemed as though the air were filled with needles, and one's body shrank involuntarily from head to foot.

Under the German gate, I saw the soldier on guard, in his great gray mantle, standing back in his box like a saint in his niche; he had his sleeve wrapped about his musket where he held it, to keep his fingers from the iron, and two long icicles hung from his moustaches. No one was on the bridge, not even the toll-gatherer, but a little further on, I saw three carts in the middle of the road with their canvas-tops all covered and glistening with frost; they were unharnessed and abandoned. Everything in the distance seemed dead; all living things had hidden themselves from the cold; and I could hear nothing but the snow crunching under my feet. Running along the cemetery, where the crosses and gravestones glistened in the snow, I said to myself: "Those who sleep there are no longer cold!" I drew my cloak over my breast, and hid my nose in the fur collar, thanking Monsieur Goulden for his lucky thought. I also thrust my hands into the muffler up to the elbows, and ran along in the deep trench, extending farther than the eye could reach, that the soldiers had made from the town as far as Quatre-Vents. On each side were walls of ice. In some places swept by the wind, I could see the oak forest and the bluish mountain, both seeming much nearer than they were, on account of the clearness of the air. Not a dog barked in a farm-yard ; it was too cold even for that.

But in spite of all this the thought of Catharine warmed my heart, and soon I descried the first houses of Quatre-Vents. The chimneys and the thatched roofs, to the right and left of the road, were scarcely higher than the mountains of snow, and the villagers had dug trenches along the walls, so that they could pass to each other's houses. But that day every family kept around its hearth, and the little round window-panes seemed painted red, from the great fires burning within. Before each door was a truss of straw to keep the cold from entering beneath it.

At the fifth door to the right I stopped to take off my mittens ; then I opened and closed it very quickly. I was at the house of Grédel Bauer, the widow of Matthias Bauer, and Catharine's mother.

As I entered, and while Aunt Grédel, seated by the hearth, astonished at my fox-skin collar, was yet turning her gray head, Catharine, in her Sunday dress—a pretty striped petticoat, a kerchief with long fringe folded across her bosom, a red apron fastened around her slender waist, a pretty cap of blue silk with black velvet bands setting off her rosy and white face, soft eyes, and rather short nose—Catharine, I say, exclaimed:

"It is Joseph!"

And without waiting to look twice, she ran to greet me, saying:

"I knew the cold would not keep you from coming."

I was so happy that I could not speak. I took off my cloak, which I hung upon a nail on the wall, with my mittens; I took off Monsieur Goulden's great shoes, and turned pale with joy.

I would have said something agreeable, but could not; suddenly I exclaimed:

"See here, Catharine; here is something for your birthday, but you must give me a kiss before opening the box."

She put up her pretty red cheek to me, and then ran to the table. Aunt Grédel also came to see the present. Catharine untied the cord and opened the box. I was behind them; my heart jumped, jumped,—I feared that the watch was not pretty enough. But in an instant, Catharine clasping her hands, said in a low voice:

"How beautiful! It is a watch!"

"Yes," said Aunt Grédel; "it is beautiful! I never saw so fine a one. One would think it was silver."

"But it *is* silver," returned Catharine, turning toward me inquiringly.

Then I said:

"Do you think, Aunt Grédel, that I would be capable of giving a gilt watch to one whom I love better than my own life? If I could do such a thing, I would despise myself more than the dirt of my shoes."

Catharine, hearing this, threw her arms around my neck; and as we stood thus, I thought: "this is the happiest day of my life." I could not let her go.

Aunt Grédel asked:

"But what is this painted upon the face?"

I could not speak to answer her; and only at last, when we were seated beside each other, I took the watch and said:

"That painting, Aunt Grédel, represents two lovers who love each other more than they can tell: Joseph Bertha and Catharine Bauer; Joseph is offering a bouquet of roses to his sweetheart, who is stretching out her hand to take them."

When Aunt Grédel had sufficiently admired the watch, she said:

"Come until I kiss you, Joseph. I see very well that you must have economized closely, and worked hard for this watch, and I think it is very pretty, and that you are a good workman, and will do us no discredit."

I kissed Aunt Grédel's cheek, and from then until midday, I did not let go Catharine's hand. We were as happy as could be looking at each other. Aunt Grédel bustled about to prepare a large pancake with dried prunes, and wine, and cinnamon, and other good things in it; but we paid no attention to her, and it was only when she put on her red jacket and black sabots, and called, "Come, my children; to table!" that we saw the fine table-cloth, the great porringer, the pitcher of wine, and the large round, golden pancake on a plate in the middle. The sight rejoiced us not a little, and Catharine said:

"Sit there, Joseph, opposite the window, that I may look at you. But you must fix my watch, for I do not know where to put it."

I passed the chain around her neck, and then, seating ourselves, we ate gayly. Without, not a sound was heard; within, the fire crackled mer-

"COME, MY CHILDREN, TO TABLE." (Page 38.)

rily upon the hearth. It was very pleasant in the large kitchen, and the gray cat, a little wild, gazed at us through the balusters of the stairs without daring to come down.

Catharine, after dinner, sang *Der liebe Gott*. She had a sweet, clear voice, and it seemed to float to heaven. I sang low, merely to sustain her. Aunt Grédel, who could never rest doing nothing, began spinning; the hum of her wheel filled up the silences, and we all felt happy. When one song was ended, we began another. At three o'clock, Aunt Grédel served up the pancake, and as we ate it, laughing, like the happiest of beings, she would exclaim:

"Come, come; now, you are children in reality."

She pretended to be angry, but we could see in her eyes that she was happy from the bottom of her heart. This lasted until four o'clock, when night began to come on apace; the darkness seemed to enter by the little windows, and, knowing that we must soon part, we sat sadly around the hearth on which the red flames were dancing. Catharine pressed my hand. I would almost have given my life to remain longer. Another half-hour passed, when Aunt Grédel cried:

"Listen, Joseph! It is time for you to go; the moon does not rise till after midnight, and it will soon be dark as a kiln outside, and an accident happens so easily in these great frosts."

These words seemed to fall like a bolt of ice, and I felt Catharine's clasp tighten on my hand. But Aunt Grédel was right.

"Come," said she, rising and taking down the cloak from the wall; "you will come again Sunday."

I had to put on the heavy shoes, the mittens, and the cloak of Monsieur Goulden, and would have wished that I were a hundred years doing so, but, unfortunately, Aunt Grédel assisted me. When I had the great collar drawn up to my ears, she said:

"Now, kiss us good-bye, Joseph."

I kissed her first, then Catharine, who did not say a word. After that I opened the door and the terrible cold, entering, admonished me not to wait.

"Hasten, Joseph," said my aunt.

"Good-night, Joseph, good-night!" cried Catharine, "and do not forget to come Sunday."

I turned round to wave my hand; and then I ran on without raising my head, for the cold was so intense that it brought tears to my eyes even behind the great collar.

I ran on thus some twenty minutes, scarcely daring to breathe, when a drunken voice called out:

"Who goes there?"

I looked through the dim night, and saw, fifty paces before me, Pinacle, the peddler, with his huge basket, his otter-skin cap, woolen gloves, and iron-pointed-staff. The lantern hanging from the strap of his basket lit up his debauched face, his chin bristling with yellow beard, and his great nose shaped like an extinguisher. He glared with his little eyes like a wolf, and repeated, "Who goes there?"

This Pinacle was the greatest rogue in the country. He had the year before a difficulty with Monsieur Goulden, who demanded of him the price of a watch which he undertook to deliver to Monsieur Anstett, the curate of Homert, and the money for which he put into his pocket, saying he paid it to me. But although the villain made oath before the justice of the peace, Monsieur Goulden knew the contrary, for on the day in question neither he nor I had left the house. Besides, Pinacle wanted to dance with Catharine at a festival at Quatre-Vents, and she refused because she knew the story of the watch, and was, besides, unwilling to leave me.

The sight, then, of this rogue with his iron-shod stick in the middle of the road did not tend to rejoice my heart. Happily a little path which wound around the cemetery was at my left, and, without replying, I dashed through it although the snow reached my waist.

Then he, guessing who I was, cried furiously:

"Aha! it is the little lame fellow! Halt! halt! I want to bid you good-evening. You came from Catharine's, you watch-stealer."

But I sprang like a hare through the heaps of snow; he at first tried to follow me, but his pack hindered him, and, when I gained the ground again, he put his hands around his mouth, and shrieked:

"Never mind, cripple, never mind! Your reckoning is coming all the same; the conscription is coming—the grand conscription of the one-eyed, the lame, and the hunch-backed. You will have to go, and you will find a place under ground like the others."

He continued his way, laughing like the sot he was, and I, scarcely able to breathe, kept on, thanking Heaven that the little alley was so near;

for Pinacle, who was known always to draw his knife in a fight, might have done me an ill turn.

In spite of my exertion, my feet, even in the thick shoes, were intensely cold, and I again began running.

That night the water froze in the cisterns of Phalsbourg and the wines in the cellars—things that had not happened before for sixty years.

On the bridge and under the German gate the silence seemed yet deeper than in the morning, and the night made it seem terrible. A few stars shone between the masses of white cloud that hung over the city. All along the street I met not a soul, and when I reached home, after shutting the door of our lower passage, it seemed warm to me, although the little stream that ran from the yard along the wall was frozen. I stopped a moment to take breath; then I ascended in the dark, my hand on the baluster.

When I opened the door of my room, the cheerful warmth of the stove was grateful indeed. Monsieur Goulden was seated in his armchair before the fire, his cap of black silk pulled over his ears, and his hands resting upon his knees.

"Is that you, Joseph?" he asked without turning round.

"It is," I answered. "How pleasant it is here, and how cold out of doors! We never had such a winter."

"No," he said gravely. "It is a winter that will long be remembered."

I went into the closet and hung the cloak and mittens in their places, and was about relating my adventure with Pinacle, when he resumed:

"You had a pleasant day of it, Joseph."

"I have had, indeed. Aunt Grédel and Catharine wished me to make you their compliments."

"Very good, very good," said he; "the young are right to amuse themselves, for when they grow old, and suffer, and see so much of injustice, selfishness, and misfortune, everything is spoiled in advance."

He spoke as if talking to himself, gazing at the fire. I had never seen him so sad, and I asked:

"Are you not well, Monsieur Goulden?"

But he, without replying, murmured:

"Yes, yes; this is to be a great military nation; this is glory!"

He shook his head and bent over gloomily, his heavy gray brows contracted in a frown.

I knew not what to think of all this, when raising his head again, he said:

"At this moment, Joseph, there are four hundred thousand families weeping in France; the grand army has perished in the snows of Russia; all those stout young men whom for two months we saw passing our gates are buried beneath them. The news came this afternoon. Oh! it is horrible! horrible!"

I was silent. Now I saw clearly that we must have another conscription, as after all campaigns, and this time the lame would most probably be called. I grew pale, and Pinacle's prophecy made my hair stand on end.

"Go to bed, Joseph; rest easy," said Monsieur Goulden. "I am not sleepy; I will stay here; all this upsets me. Did you remark anything in the city?"

"No, Monsieur Goulden."

I went to my room and to bed. For a long time I could not close my eyes, thinking of the conscription, of Catharine, and of so many thousands of men buried in the snow, and then I plotted flight to Switzerland.

About three o'clock Monsieur Goulden retired, and a few minutes after, through God's grace, I fell asleep.

IV.

WHEN I arose in the morning, about seven, I went to Monsieur Goulden's room to begin work; but he was still in bed, looking weary and sick.

"Joseph," said he, "I am not well. This horrible news has made me ill, and I have not slept at all."

"Shall I not make you some tea?" I asked.

"No, my child, that is not worth while. I will get up by and by. But this is the day to regulate the city clocks; I cannot go; for to see so many good people—people I have known for thirty years—in misery, would kill me. Listen, Joseph: take those keys hanging behind the door, and go. I will try to sleep a little. If I could sleep an hour or two, it would do me good."

"Very well, Monsieur Goulden," I replied; "I will go at once."

After putting more wood in the stove, I took the cloak and mittens, drew Monsieur Goulden's bed-curtains, and went out, the bunch of keys in my pocket. The illness of Father Melchior grieved me very much for a while, but a thought came to console me, and I said to myself: "You can climb up the city clock-tower, and see the house of Catharine and Aunt Grédel." Thinking thus, I arrived at the house of Brainstein, the bell-ringer, who lived at the corner of the little place, in an old, tumble-down barrack. His two sons were weavers, and in their old home the noise of the loom and the whistle of the shuttle was heard from morning till night. The grandmother, old and blind, slept in an arm-chair, on the back of which perched a magpie. Father Brainstein, when he did not have to ring the bells for a christening, a funeral, or a marriage, kept reading his almanac behind the small round panes of his window.

Beside their hut was a little box under the roof of the old hall, where the cobbler Koniam worked, and further on were the butchers' and fruiterers' shops.

I came then to Brainstein's, and the old man, when he saw me, rose up, saying:

"It is you, Monsieur Joseph."

"Yes, Father Brainstein; I come in place of Monsieur Goulden, who is not well."

"Very good; it is all the same."

He took up his staff and put on his woolen cap, driving away the cat that was sleeping upon it; then he took the great key of the steeple from a drawer, and we went out together, I glad to find myself again in the open air, despite the cold; for their miserable room was gray with vapor, and as hard to breathe in as a kettle; I could never understand how people could live in such a way.

At last we gained the street, and Father Brainstein said:

"You have heard of the great Russian disaster, Monsieur Joseph?"

"Yes, Father Brainstein; it is fearful!"

"Ah!" said he, "there will be many a Mass said in the churches; every one will weep and pray for their children, the more that they are dead in a heathen land."

"Certainly, certainly," I replied.

We crossed the court, and in front of the tower-hall, opposite the guard-house, many peasants and city people were already standing, reading a placard. We went up the steps and entered the church, where more than twenty women, young and old, were kneeling on the pavement, in spite of the terrible cold.

"Is it not as I said?" said Brainstein. "They are coming already to pray, and half of them have been here since five o'clock."

He opened the little door of the steeple leading to the organ, and we began climbing up in the dark. Once in the organ-loft, we turned to the left of the bellows, and went up to the bells.

I was glad to see the blue sky and breathe the free air again, for the bad odor of the bats which inhabited the tower almost suffocated me. But how terrible the cold was in that cage, open to every wind, and how dazzlingly the snow shone over twenty leagues of country! All the little city of Phalsbourg, with its six bastions, three *demilunes*, two advanced works, its barracks, magazines, bridges, *glacis*, ramparts; its great parade-ground, and little, well-aligned houses, were beneath me, as if drawn on white paper. I was not yet accustomed to the height, and I held fast on the middle of the platform for fear I might jump off, for I had read of people having their heads turned by great heights. I did not dare go to the clock, and, if Brainstein had not set me the example, I would have remained there, pressed against the beam from which the bells hung: but he said:

"Come, Monsieur Joseph, and see if it is right."

Then I took out Monsieur Goulden's large watch which marked seconds, and I saw that the clock was considerably slow. Brainstein helped me to wind it up, and we regulated it.

"The clock is always slow in winter," said he, "because of the iron working."

After becoming somewhat accustomed to the elevation, I began to look around. There were the Oakwood barracks, the upper barracks, Bigelberg, and lastly, opposite me, Quatre-Vents, and the house of Aunt Grédel, from the chimney of which a thread of blue smoke rose toward the sky. And I saw the kitchen, and imagined Catharine, in sabots, and woolen skirt, spinning at the corner of the hearth and thinking of me. I no longer felt the cold; I could not take my eyes from their cottage.

Father Brainstein, who did not know what I was looking at, said:

"Yes, yes, Monsieur Joseph: now all the roads are covered with people in spite of the snow. The news has already spread, and every one wants to know the extent of his loss."

He was right; every road and path was covered with people coming to the city; and looking in the court, I saw the crowd increasing every moment before the guard-house, the town-house, and the post-office. A deep murmur arose from the mass.

At length, after a last, long look at Catharine's house, I had to descend, and we went down the dark, winding stairs, as if descending into a well. Once in the organ-loft, we saw that the crowd had greatly increased in the church; all the mothers, the sisters, the old grandmothers, the rich, and the poor, were kneeling on the benches in the midst of the deepest silence; they prayed for the absent, offering all only to see them once again.

At first I did not realize all this; but suddenly the thought that, if I had gone the year before, Catharine would be there, praying and asking me of God, fell like a bolt on my heart, and I felt all my body tremble.

"Let us go! let us go!" I exclaimed, "this is terrible."

"What is?" he asked.

"War."

We descended the stairs under the great gate,

and I went across the court to the house of Monsieur the Commandant Meunier, while Brainstein took the way to his house.

At the corner of the Hotel de Ville, I saw a sight which I shall remember all my life. There, around a placard, were more than five hundred people, men and women crowded against each other, all pale, and with necks outstretched, gazing at it as at some horrible apparition. They could not read it, and from time to time one would say in German or French:

"But they are not all dead! Some will return."

Others cried out:

"Let us see it! let us get near it."

A poor old woman in the rear lifted up her hands, and cried:

"Christopher! my poor Christopher!"

Others, angry at her clamor, called out:

"Keep that old woman quiet."

Each one thought only of himself.

Behind, the crowd continued to pour through the German gate.

At length, Harmantier, the *sergent-de-ville*, came out of the guard-house, and stood at the top of the steps, with another placard like the first; a few soldiers followed him. Then a rush was made toward him, but the soldiers kept off the crowd, and old Harmantier began to read the placard, which he called the twenty-ninth bulletin, and in which the Emperor informed them that during the retreat the horses perished every night by thousands. He said nothing of the men!

The *sergent-de-ville* read slowly; not a breath was heard in the crowd; even the old woman, who did not understand French, listened like the others. The buzz of a fly could have been heard. But when he came to this passage, "Our cavalry was dismounted to such an extent that we were forced to bring together the officers who yet owned horses to form four companies of one hundred and fifty men each. Generals rated as captains, and colonels as under-officers"—when he read this passage, which told more of the misery of the grand army than all the rest, cries and groans arose on all sides; two or three women fell and were carried away.

It is true that the bulletin added, "The health of his majesty was never better," and that was a great consolation. Unfortunately it could not restore life to three hundred thousand men buried in the snow; and so the people went away very sad. Others came by dozens who had not heard the news read, and from time to time Harmantier came out to read the bulletin.

This lasted until night; still the same scene over and over again.

I ran from the place; I wanted to know nothing about it.

I went to Monsieur the Commandant's. Entering a parlor, I saw him at breakfast. He was an old man, but hale, with a red face and good appetite.

"Ah! it is you!" said he, "Monsieur Goulden is not coming, then?"

"No, Monsieur the Commandant, the bad news has made him ill."

"Ah! I understand," he said, emptying his glass; "yes, it is unfortunate."

And while I was regulating the clock, he added:

"Well! tell Monsieur Goulden that we will have our revenge. We cannot always have the upper hand. For fifteen years we have kept the drums beating over them, and it is only right to let them have this little morsel of consolation. And then our honor is safe; we were not beaten fighting; without the cold and the snow, those poor Cossacks would have had a hard time of it. But patience; the skeletons of our regiments will soon be filled, and then let them beware."

I wound up the clock; he rose and came to look at it, for he was a great amateur in clockmaking. He pinched my ear in a merry mood; and then, as I was going away, he cried as he buttoned up his overcoat, which he had opened before beginning breakfast:

"Tell Father Goulden to rest easy; the dance will begin again in the spring; the Kalmucks will not always have winter fighting for them. Tell him that."

"Yes, Monsieur the Commandant," I answered, shutting the door.

His burly figure and air of good humor comforted me a little; but in all the other houses I went to, at the Horwiches, the Frantz-Tonis, the Durlaches, everywhere I heard only lamentations. The women especially were in misery; the men said nothing, but walked about with heads hanging down, and without even looking to see what I was doing.

Toward ten o'clock there only remained two persons for me to see: Monsieur de la Vablerie-Chamberlan, one of the ancient nobility, who lived at the end of the main street, with Madame Chamberlan-d'Ecof and Mademoiselle Jeanne, their daughter. They were *émigrés*, and had returned about three or four years before. They saw no one in the city, and only three or four old priests in the environs. Monsieur de la Vablerie-Chamberlan loved only the chase. He had six dogs at the end of the yard, and a two-horse carriage; Father Robert, of the Rue des Capucins, served them as coachman, groom, footman, and huntsman. Monsieur de la Vablerie-Chamberlan always wore a hunting vest, a leathern cap, and boots and spurs. All the town called him the hunter, but they said nothing of Madame nor of Mademoiselle de Chamberlan.

I was very sad when I pushed open the heavy door, which closed with a pulley whose creaking echoed through the vestibule. What was then my surprise to hear, in the midst of general mourning, the tones of a song and harpsichord! Monsieur de la Vablerie was singing, and Mademoiselle Jeanne accompanying him. I knew not, in those days, that the misfortune of one was often the joy of others, and I said to myself with my hand on the latch: "They have not heard the news from Russia."

But while I stood thus, the door of the kitchen opened, and Mademoiselle Louise, their servant, putting out her head, asked:

"Who is there?"

"It is I, Mademoiselle Louise."

"Ah! it is you, Monsieur Joseph. Come this way."

They had their clock in a large parlor which they rarely entered; the high windows, with blinds, remained closed; but there was light enough for what I had to do. I passed then through the kitchen and regulated the antique clock, which was a magnificent piece of work of white marble. Mademoiselle Louise looked on.

"You have company, Mademoiselle Louise?" said I.

"No, but monsieur ordered me to let no one in."

"You are very cheerful here."

"Ah! yes," she said; "and it is for the first time in years; I don't know what is the matter."

My work done, I left the house, meditating on these occurrences, which seemed to me strange. The idea never entered my mind that they were rejoicing at our defeat.

Then I turned the corner of the street to go to Father Féral's, who was called the "Standard-bearer," because, at the age of forty-five, he, a blacksmith, and for many years the father of a family, had carried the colors of the volunteers of Phalsbourg in '92, and only returned after the Zurich campaign. He had his three sons in the army of Russia, Jean, Louis, and George Féral. George was commandant of dragoons; the two others, officers of infantry.

I imagined the grief of Father Féral while I was going, but it was nothing to what I saw when I entered his room. The poor old man, blind and bald, was sitting in an arm-chair behind the stove, his head bowed upon his breast, and his sightless eyes open, and staring as if he saw his three sons stretched at his feet. He did not speak, but great drops of sweat rolled down his forehead on his long, thin cheeks, while his face was pale as that of a corpse. Four or five of his old comrades of the times of the Republic—Father Desmarets, Father Nivoi, old Paradis, and tall old Froissard—had come to console him. They sat around him in silence, smoking their pipes, and looking as if they themselves needed comfort.

From time to time one or the other would say:

"Come, come, Féral! are we no longer veterans of the army of the Sambre-and-Meuse?"

Or,

"Courage, Standard-bearer: courage! Did we not carry the battery at Fleurus?"

Or some other similar remark.

But he did not reply; every minute he sighed, his aged, hollow cheeks swelled; then he leaned over, and the old friends made signs to each other, shaking their heads, as if to say:

"This looks bad."

I hastened to regulate the clock and depart, for to see the poor old man in such a plight made my heart bleed.

When I arrived at home, I found Monsieur Goulden at his work-bench.

"You are returned, Joseph," said he. "Well?"

"Well, Monsieur Goulden, you had reason to stay away; it is terrible."

And I told him all in detail.

"Yes; I knew it all," said he, sadly, "but our misfortunes are only beginning; these Prussians and Austrians and Russians and Spaniards—all the nations we have been beating since eighteen hundred and four, are now taking advantage of our ill luck to fall upon us. We gave them kings and queens they did not know from Adam nor Eve, and whom they did not want, it seems, and now they are going to bring back the old ones with all their trains of nobles, and after pouring out our blood for the Emperor's brothers, we are about losing all we gained by the Revolution. Instead of being first among the first, we will be last among the last. While you were away I was thinking of all this; it is unavoidable—We relied upon soldiers alone, and now that we have no more, we are nothing."

He arose. I set the table, and, whilst we were dining in silence, the bells of the steeples began to ring.

"Some one is dead in the city," said Monsieur Goulden.

"Indeed? I did not hear of it."

Ten minutes after, the Rabbi Rose came in to have a glass put in his watch.

"Who is dead?" asked Monsieur Goulden.

"Poor old Standard-bearer."

"What! Father Féral?"

"Yes, near an hour ago. Father Demarets and several others tried to comfort him; at last he asked them to read to him the last letter of his son George, the commandant of dragoons, in which he says that next spring he hoped to embrace his father with a colonel's epaulettes. As the old man heard this, he tried to rise, but fell back with his head upon his knees. That letter had broken his heart."

Monsieur Goulden made no remark on the news.

"Here is your watch, Monsieur Rose," said he, handing it back to the rabbi; "it is twelve sous."

Monsieur Rose departed, and we finished our dinner in silence.

V

A few days after, the gazette announced that the Emperor was in Paris, and that the King of Rome and the Empress Marie-Louise were about to be crowned. Monsieur the Mayor, his co-adjutor and the municipal councillors now spoke only of the rights of the throne, and Professor Burguet, the elder, wrote a speech on the subject which Baron Parmentier read. But all this produced but little effect on the people, because every one was afraid of being carried off by the conscription, and knew that many more soldiers were needed; all were in trouble, and I grew thinner day by day. In vain would Monsieur Goulden say: "Fear nothing, Joseph; you cannot march. Consider, my child, that any one as lame as you would give out at the end of the first mile."

But all this did not lessen my uneasiness.

Monsieur Goulden, often, too, when we were alone at work, would say to me:

"If those who are now masters, and who tell us that God placed them here on earth to make us happy, would foresee at the beginning of a campaign the poor old men, the hapless mothers, whose very hearts they have torn away to satisfy their pride—if they could see the tears and hear the groans of these poor people when they are coldly told 'Your son is dead; you will see him no more; he perished, crushed by horses' hoofs, or torn to pieces by a cannon-ball, or died mayhap afar off in a hospitial, after having his arm or leg cut off,—burning with fever, without one kind word to console him, but calling for his parents as when he was an infant,'—if, I say, these haughty ones of earth could thus see the tears of those mothers, I do not believe that one among them would be barbarous enough to continue the war. But they think nothing of this; they think other folks do not love their children as they love theirs; they think people are no more than beasts. They are wrong; all their great genius, their lofty notions of glory, are as nothing, for there is only one thing for which a people should fly to arms—men, women, children—old and young. It is when their liberty is assailed as ours was in '92—then all should die or conquer together; he who remains behind is a coward, who would have others fight for him;—the victory then is not for a few, but for all;—then sons and fathers are defending their families; if they are killed, it is a misfortune, to be sure, but they die for their rights. Such a man, Joseph, is the only just one, the one of which no one can complain; all others are shameful, and the glory they bring is not glory fit for a man, but only for a wild beast."

On the eighth of January, a huge placard was posted on the town-hall, stating that the Emperor would levy, after a *senatus-consultus*, as they said in those days, in the first place, one hundred and fifty thousand conscripts of 1813; then one hundred *cohortes* of the first call of 1812 who thought they had already escaped; then one hundred thousand conscripts of from 1809 to 1812, and so on to the end; so that every loophole was closed, and we would have a larger army than before the Russian expedition.

When Father Fouze, the glazier, came to us with this news, one morning, I almost fell, through faintness, for I thought:

"Now they will take all, even fathers of families. I am lost!"

Monsieur Goulden poured some water on my neck; my arms hung useless by my side; I was pale as a corpse.

But I was not the only one upon whom the placard had such an effect: that year many young men refused to go; some broke their teeth off, so as not to be able to tear the cartridge; others blew off their thumbs with pistols, so as not to be able to hold a musket; others, again, fled to the woods; they proclaimed them "refractories," but they had not *gendarmes* enough to capture them.

The mothers of families took courage to revolt after a manner, and to encourage their sons not to obey the *gendarmes*. They aided them in every way; they cried out against the Emperor, and the clergy of all denominations sustained them in so doing. The cup was at last full!

The very day of the proclamation I went to Quatre-Vents; but it was not now in the joy of my heart; it was as the most miserable of unhappy wretches, about to be bereft of love and life. I could scarcely walk, and when I reached there I did not know how to announce the evil tidings; but I saw at a glance that they knew all, for Catharine was weeping bitterly, and Aunt Grédel was pale with indignation.

We embraced in silence, and the first words Aunt Grédel said to me, as in her anger she pushed her grey hair behind her ears, were:

"You shall not go! What have we to do with wars? The priest himself told us it was at last too much, and that we ought to have peace! You shall not go! Do not cry, Catharine; I say he shall not go!"

She was fairly green with anger, and rattled her kettles noisily together, saying:

"This carnage has lasted long enough. Our two poor cousins, Kasper and Yokel, are already going to lose their lives in Spain for this Emperor, and now he comes to ask us for the younger ones. He is not satisfied to have slain three hundred thousand in Russia. Instead of thinking of peace, like a man of sense, he thinks only of massacring the few who remain. We will see! We will see!"

"In the name of Heaven! Aunt Grédel, be quiet; speak lower," said I, looking at the window. "If they hear you, we are lost."

"I speak for them to hear me," she replied.

"Your Napoleon does not frighten me. He commenced by closing our mouths, so that he might do as he pleased; but the end approaches. Four young women are losing their husbands in our village alone, and ten poor young men are forced to abandon everything, despite father, mother, religion, justice, God! Is not this horrible?"

I tried to answer, but she kept on:

"Hold, Joseph," said she; "be silent; your Emperor has no heart—he will end miserably yet. God showed his finger this winter; He saw that we feared a man more then we feared Him; that mothers—like those whose babes Herod slew—dared no longer cling to their own flesh when that man demanded them for massacre; and so the cold came and our army perished; and now those who are leaving us are the same as already dead. God is weary of all this! You shall not go!" cried she obstinately; "I shall not let you go; you shall fly to the woods with Jean Kraft, Louise Bême, and all our bravest fellows; you shall go to the mountains—to Switzerland, and Catharine and I will go with you and remain until this destruction of men is ended."

Then Aunt Grédel became silent. Instead of giving us an ordinary dinner, she gave us a better one than on Catharine's birthday, and said, with the air of one who has taken a resolution:

"Eat, my children, and fear not; there will soon be a change!"

I returned about four in the evening to Phalsbourg, somewhat calmer than when I set out. But as I went up the Rue de la Munitionnaire, I heard at the corner of the college the drum of the *sergent-de-ville*, Harmantier, and I saw a throng gathered around him. I ran to hear what was going on, and I arrived just as he began reading a proclamation.

Harmantier read that, by the *senatus-consultus* of the 3d, the drawing for the conscription would take place on the 15th.

It was already the 8th, and only seven days remained. This upset me completely.

The crowd dispersed in the deepest silence. I went home sad enough, and said to Monsieur Goulden:

"The drawing takes place next Thursday."

"Ah!" he exclaimed, "they are losing no time; things are pressing."

It is easy to imagine my grief that day and the days following. I could scarcely stand; I constantly saw myself on the point of leaving home. I saw myself flying to the woods, the *gendarmes* at my heels, crying, "Halt! halt!" Then I thought of the misery of Catharine, of Aunt Grédel, of Monsieur Goulden. Then I imagined myself marching in the ranks with a number of other wretches, to whom they were crying out, "Forward! charge bayonets!" while whole files were being swept away. I heard bullets whistle and shells shriek; in a word, I was in a pitiable state.

"Be calm, Joseph," said Monsieur Goulden; "do not torment yourself thus. I think that of all who may be drawn there are probably not ten who can give as good reasons as you for staying at home. The surgeon must be blind to receive you. Besides, I will see Monsieur the Commandant. Calm yourself."

But these kind words could not reassure me.

Thus I passed an entire week almost in a trance, and when the day of the drawing arrived, Thursday morning, I was so pale, so sick-looking, that the parents of conscripts envied, so to speak, my appearance for their sons. "That fellow," they said, "has a chance; he would drop the first mile. Some people are born under a lucky star!"

VI.

THE town-house of Phalsbourg, that Thursday morning, January 15th, 1813, during the drawing of the conscription, was a sight to be seen. To-day it is bad enough to be drawn, to be forced to have parents, friends, home, one's cattle and one's fields, to go and learn—God knows where—"*One! two!* one! two! halt! eyes left! eyes right! front! carry arms!" etc. etc. Yes, this is all bad enough, but there is a chance of returning. One can say, with something like confidence: "In seven years I shall see my old nest again, and my parents, and perhaps my sweetheart. I shall have seen the world, and will perhaps have some title to be appointed forester or gendarme." This is a comfort for reasonable people. But *then*, if you had the ill-luck to lose in the lottery, there was an end of you often not one in a hundred returned. The idea that you were only going for a time never entered your head.

The enrolled of Harberg, of Garbourg, and of Quatre-Vents were to draw first; then those of the city, and lastly those of Wéchem and Mittelbronn.

I was up early in the morning, and with my elbows on the work-bench I watched the people pass by; young men in blouses, poor old men in cotton caps and short vests; old women in jackets and woolen shirts, bent almost double, with a staff or umbrella under their arms. They arrived by families. Monsieur the Sub-Prefect of Sarrebourg, with his silver collar, and his secretary, had stopped the day before at the "Red Ox," and they were also looking out of the window. Toward eight o'clock, Monsieur Goulden began work, after breakfasting. I ate nothing, but stared and stared until Monsieur the Mayor Parmentier and his coadjutor, came for Monsieur the Sub-Prefect.

The drawing began at nine, and soon we heard the clarionet of Pfifer-Karl and the violin of big Andrès resounding through the streets. They were playing the "March of the Swedes," an

"QUI VIVE!" (Page 74.)

air to which thousands of poor wretches had left old Alsace for ever. The conscripts danced, linked arms, shouted until their voices seemed to pierce the clouds, stamped on the ground, waved their hats, trying to seem joyful while death was at their hearts. Well, it was the fashion; and big Andrès, withered, stiff, and yellow as boxwood, and his short chubby comrade, with cheeks extended to their utmost tension, seemed like people who would lead you to the church-yard all the while chatting indifferently.

That music, those cries, sent a shudder through my heart.

I had just put on my swallow tailed coat and my beaver hat, to go out, when Aunt Grédel and Catharine entered, saying:

"Good-morning, Monsieur Goulden. We have come for the conscription."

Then I saw how Catharine had been crying. Her eyes were red, and she threw her arms around my neck, while her mother turned to me.

Monsieur Goulden said:

"It will soon be the turn of the young men of the town."

"Yes, Monsieur Goulden," answered Catharine,

in a choking voice; "they have finished Harberg."

"Then it is time for you to go, Joseph," said he; "but do not grieve; do not be frightened. These drawings, you know, are only a matter of form. For a long while past none can escape; for if they escape one drawing, they are caught a year or two after. All the numbers are bad. When the council of exemption meets, we will see what is best to be done. To-day it is merely a sort of satisfaction they give the people to draw in the lottery; but every one loses."

"No matter," said Aunt Grédel; "Joseph will win."

"Yes, yes," replied Monsieur Goulden, smiling, "he cannot fail."

Then I sallied forth with Catharine and Aunt Grédel, and we went to the town square, where the crowd was. In all the shops, dozens of conscripts, purchasing ribbons, thronged around the counters, weeping and singing as if possessed. Others in the inns embraced, sobbing; but still they sang. Two or three musicians of the neighborhood—the Gipsy Walteufel, Rosselkasten, and George Adam—had arrived, and their pieces thundered in terrible and heart-rending strains.

Catharine squeezed my arm. Aunt Grédel followed.

Opposite the guard-house I saw the peddler Pinacle afar off, his pack opened on a little table, and beside it a long pole decked with ribbons which he was selling to the conscripts.

I hastened to pass by him, when he cried:

"Ha! Cripple! Halt! Come here; I have a ribbon for you; you must have a magnificent one—one to draw a prize by."

He waved a long black ribbon above his head, and I grew pale despite myself. But as we ascended the steps of the town-house, a conscript was just descending; it was Klipfel, the smith of the French gate; he had drawn number eight, and shouted:

"The black for me, Pinacle! Bring it here, whatever may happen."

His face was gloomy, but he laughed. His little brother Jean was crying behind him, and said:

"No, no, Jacob! not the black!"

But Pinacle fastened the ribbon to the smith's hat, while the latter said:

"That is what we want now. We are all dead, and should wear our own mourning."

And he cried savagely:

"*Vive l'Empereur!*"

I was better satisfied to see the black ribbon on his hat than on mine, and I slipped quickly through the crowd to avoid Pinacle.

We had great difficulty in getting into the town-house and in climbing the old oak stairs, where people were going up and down in swarms. In the great hall above, the gendarme Kelz walked about maintaining order as well as he could, and in the council-chamber at the side, where there was a painting of Justice with her eyes blindfolded, we heard them calling off the numbers. From time to time a conscript came out with flushed face, fastening his number to his cap and passing with bowed head through the crowd, like a furious bull who cannot see clearly and who would seem to wish to break his horns against the walls. Others, on the contrary, passed as pale as death. The windows of the town-house were open, and without we heard six or seven pieces playing together. It was horrible.

I pressed Catharine's hand, and we passed slowly through the crowd to the hall where Monsieur the Sub-Prefect, the Mayors, and the Secretaries were seated on their tribune, calling the numbers aloud, as if pronouncing sentence of death in a court of justice, for all these numbers were really sentences of death.

We waited a long while.

It seemed as if there was no longer a drop of blood in my veins, when at last my name was called.

I stepped up, seeing and hearing nothing; I put my hand in the box and drew a number.

Monsieur the Sub-Prefect cried out:

"Number seventeen."

Then I left without speaking, Catharine and her mother behind me. We went out into the square, and, the air reviving me, I remembered that I had drawn number seventeen.

Aunt Grédel seemed confounded.

"And I put something into your pocket, too," said she; "but that rascal of a Pinacle gave you ill luck.

At the same time she drew from my coat-pocket the end of a cord. Great drops of sweat rolled down my forehead; Catharine was white as marble, and so we went back to Monsieur Goulden's.

"What number did you draw, Joseph?" he asked, as soon as he saw us.

"Seventeen," replied Aunt Grédel, sitting down with her hands upon her knees.

Monsieur Goulden seemed troubled for a moment, but he said instantly:

"One is as good as another. All will go; the skeletons must be filled. But it don't matter for Joseph. I will go and see Monsieur the Mayor and Monsieur the Commandant. It will be telling no lie to say that Joseph is lame; all the town knows that; but among so many they may overlook him. That is why I go, so rest easy; do not be anxious."

These words of good Monsieur Goulden reassured Aunt Grédel and Catharine, who returned to Quatre-Vents full of hope; but they did not affect me, for from that moment I had not a moment of rest day or night.

The Emperor had a good custom: he did not allow the conscripts to languish at home. Soon as the drawing was complete, the council of revision met, and a few days after came the orders of march. He did not do like those tooth-pullers who first show you their pincers and hooks and gaze for an hour into your mouth, so that you feel half dead before they make up their minds to begin work: he proceeded without loss of time.

A week after the drawing, the council of revision sat at the town-hall, with all the mayors and a few notables of the country to give advice in case of need.

The day before Monsieur Goulden had put on his brown great-coat and his best wig to go to wind up Monsieur the Mayor's clock and that of the Commandant. He returned laughing and said:

"All goes well, Joseph. Monsieur the Mayor and Monsieur the Commandant know that you are lame; that is easy enough to be seen. They replied at once, Eh, Monsieur Goulden, the young man is lame; why speak of him? Do not be uneasy; we do not want the infirm; we want soldiers."

These words poured balm on my wounds, and that night I slept like one of the blessed. But the next day fear again assailed me; I remembered suddenly how many men full of defects had gone all the same, and how many others invented defects to deceive the council; for instance, swallowing injurious substances to make them pale; tying up their legs to give themselves swollen veins; or playing deaf, blind, or foolish. Thinking over all these things, I trembled at not being lame enough, and determined that I would appear sufficiently forlorn. I had heard that vinegar would make one sick, and, without telling Monsieur Goulden, in my fear I swallowed all the vinegar in his bottle. Then I dressed myself, thinking that I looked like a dead man, for the vinegar was very strong; but when I entered Monsieur Goulden's room, he cried out:

"Joseph, what is the matter with you? You are as red as a cock's comb."

And, looking at myself in the mirror, I saw that my face was red to my ears, and to the tip of my nose. I was frightened, but instead of growing pale I became redder yet, and I cried out in my distress:

"Now I am lost indeed! I will seem like a man without a single defect, and full of health. The vinegar is rushing to my head.

"What vinegar?" asked Monsieur Goulden.

"That in your bottle. I drank it to make myself pale, as they say Mademoiselle Sclapp, the organist, does. O heavens! what a fool I was."

"That does not prevent your being lame," said Monsieur Goulden; "but you tried to deceive the council, which was dishonest. But it is half-past nine, and Werner is come to tell me you must be there at ten o'clock. So, hurry."

I had to go in that state; the heat of the vinegar seemed bursting from my cheeks, and when I met Catharine and her mother, who were waiting for me at the town-house, they scarcely knew me.

"How happy and satisfied you look!" said Aunt Grédel.

I would have fainted on hearing this if the vinegar had not sustained me in spite of myself. I went up-stairs in terrible agony, without being able to move my tongue to reply, so great was the horror I felt at my folly.

Up stairs, more than twenty-five conscripts who pretended to be infirm, had been examined and received, while twenty-five others, on a bench along the wall, sat with drooping heads awaiting their turn.

The old gendarme, Kelz, with his huge cocked hat, was walking about, and as soon as he saw me, exclaimed:

"At last! At last! Here is one, at all events, who will not be sorry to go; the love of glory is shining in his eyes. Very good, Joseph; I predict that at the end of the campaign you will be corporal."

"But I am lame," I cried, angrily.

"Lame!" repeated Kelz, winking and smiling; "lame! No matter. With such health as yours you can always hold your own."

He had scarcely ceased speaking when the door of the hall of the Council of Revision opened, and the other gendarme, Werner, putting out his head, called me by name, "Joseph Bertha."

I entered, limping as much as I could, and Werner shut the door. The mayors of the canton were seated in a semi-circle, Monsieur the Sub-Prefect and the Mayor of Phalsbourg in the middle, in arm-chairs, and the Secretary Freylig at his table. A Harberg conscript was dressing himself, the gendarme Descarmes helping him put on his suspenders. This conscript, with a mass of brown hair falling over his eyes, his neck bare, and his mouth open as he caught his breath, seemed like a man going to be hanged. Two surgeons—the Surgeon-in-Chief of the Hospital, with another in uniform—were conversing in the middle of the hall. They turned to me, saying, "Undress yourself."

I did so, even to my shirt. The others looked on.

Monsieur the Sub-Prefect observed:

'There is a young man full of health."

These words angered me, but I nevertheless replied respectfully:

"I am lame, Monsieur the Sub-Prefect."

The surgeon examined me, and the one from the hospital, to whom Monsieur the Commandant had doubtless spoken of me, said:

"The left leg is a little short."

"Bah!" said the other; "it is sound."

Then placing his hand upon my chest he said, "The conformation is good. Cough."

I coughed as feebly as I could; but he found me all right, and said again:

"Look at his color. How good his blood must be!"

Then I, seeing that they would pass me if I remained silent, replied:

"I have been drinking vinegar."

"Ah!" said he; that proves you have a good stomach; you like vinegar."

"But I am lame!" I cried in my distress.

"Bah! don't grieve at that," he answered; "your leg is sound. I'll answer for it."

"But that," said Monsieur the Mayor, "does not prevent his being lame from birth; all Phalsbourg knows that."

"The leg is too short," said the surgeon from

the hospital; "it is doubtless a case for exemption."

"Yes," said the Mayor; "I am sure that this young man could not endure a long march; he would drop on the road the second mile."

The first surgeon said nothing more.

I thought myself saved, when Monsieur the Sub-Prefect asked:

"You are really Joseph Bertha?"

"Yes, Monsieur the Sub-Prefect," I answered.

"Well, gentlemen," said he, taking a letter out of his portfolio, "listen."

He began to read the letter, which stated that, six months before, I had bet that I could go to Laverne and back quicker than Pinacle; that we had run the race, and I had won.

It was unhappily too true. The villain Pinacle had always taunted me with being a cripple, and in my anger I laid the wager. Every one knew of it. I could not deny it.

While I stood utterly confounded, the first surgeon said:

"That settles the question. Dress yourself." And turning to the secretary, he cried, "Good for service."

I took up my coat in despair.

Werner called another. I no longer saw anything. Some one helped me to get my arms in my coat-sleeves. Then I found myself upon the stairs, and while Catharine asked me what had passed, I sobbed aloud and would have fallen from top to bottom if Aunt Grédel had not supported me.

We went out by the rear-way and crossed the little court. I wept like a child, and Catharine did too. Out in the hall, in the shadow, we stopped to embrace each other.

Aunt Grèdel cried out:

"Oh the robbers! They are taking the lame and the sick. It is all the same to them; next they will take us."

A crowd began collecting, and Sépel the butcher, who was cutting meat in the stall, said:

"Mother Grédel, in the name of heaven keep quiet. They will put you in prison."

"Well, let them put me there!" she cried, "let them murder me. I say that men are fools to allow such outrages!"

But the *sergent-de-ville* was coming up, and we went on together weeping. We turned the corner of Café Hemmerle, and went into our own house. People looked at us from the windows and said, "There is another one who is going."

Monsieur Goulden knowing that Aunt Grédel and Catharine would come to dine with us the day of the revision, had had a stuffed goose and two bottles of good Alsace wine sent from the "Golden Sheep." He was sure that I would be exempted at once. What was his surprise, then, to see us enter together in such distress.

"What is the matter?" said he, raising his silk cap over his bald forehead, and staring at us with eyes wide open.

I had not strength enough to answer. I threw myself into the arm-chair and burst into tears. Catharine sat down beside me, and our sobs redoubled.

Aunt Grédel said:

"The robbers have taken him."

"It is not possible!" exclaimed Monsieur Goulden, letting fall his arms by his side.

"It shows their villainy," replied my aunt, and growing more and more excited, she cried, "Will a revolution never come again? Shall those wretches always be our masters?"

"Calm yourself, Mother Grédel," said Monsieur Goulden. "In the name of Heaven don't cry so loud. Joseph, tell me how it happened. They are surely mistaken; it cannot be otherwise. Did Monsieur the Mayor and the hospital surgeon say nothing?"

I told the history of the letter between my sobs, and Aunt Grédel, who until then knew nothing of it, again shrieked with her hands clenched.

"O the scoundrel! God grant that he may cross my threshold again. I will cleave his head with my hatchet."

Monsieur Goulden was astounded.

"And you did not say that it was false. Then the story was true?"

And as I bowed my head without replying, he clasped his hands, saying:

"O youth! youth! it thinks of nothing. What folly! what folly!"

He walked around the room; then sat down to wipe his spectacles, and Aunt Grédel exclaimed:

"Yes, but they shall not have him yet! Their wickedness shall yet go for nothing. This very evening Joseph shall be in the mountains on the way to Switzerland."

Monsieur Goulden hearing this, looked grave; he bent his brows, and replied in a few moments:

"It is a misfortune, a great misfortune, for Joseph is really lame. They will yet find it out, for he cannot march two days without falling behind and becoming sick. But you are wrong, Mother Grédel, to speak as you do and give him bad advice."

"Bad advice!" she cried. "Then you are for having people massacred too!"

"No," he answered; "I do not love wars, especially where a hundred thousand men lose their lives for the glory of one. But wars of that kind are ended. It is not now for glory and to win new kingdoms that soldiers are levied, but to defend our country, which had been put in danger by tyranny and ambition. We would gladly have peace now. Unhappily, the Russians are advancing; the Prussians are joining them: and our friends, the Austrians, only await a good opportunity to fall upon our rear. If we do not go to meet them, they will come to our homes; for we are about to have Europe on our hands as we had in '93. It is now a different matter from our wars in Spain, in Russia, and in Germany; and I, old as I am, Mother Grédel, if the danger continues to increase and the veterans of the republic are needed, I would be ashamed to go and make clocks in Switzerland while others were pouring out their blood to defend my country. Besides, remember this well, that deserters are despised everywhere; after having committed such an act, they have no kindred or home anywhere. They have neither father, mother, church nor country. They are incapable of fulfilling the first duty of man—to love and sustain their country, even though she be in the wrong."

He said no more at the moment, but sat gravely down.

"Let us eat," he exclaimed, after some minutes of silence. "It is striking twelve o'clock." Mother Grédel and Catharine, seat yourselves there."

They sat down, and we began dinner. I thought of the words of Monsieur Goulden, which seemed right to me. Aunt Grédel compressed her lips, and from time to time gazed at me as if to read my thoughts. At length she said:

"I despise a country where they take fathers of families after carrying off the sons. If I were in Joseph's place, I would fly at once."

"Listen, Aunt Grédel," I replied; "you know that I love nothing so much as peace and quiet but I would not, nevertheless, run away like a coward to another country. But, notwithstanding, I will do as Catharine says; if she wishes me to go to Switzerland, I will go."

Then Catharine, lowering her head to hide her tears, said in a low voice:

"I would not have them call you a deserter."

"Well, then, I will do like the others," I cried; "and as those of Phalsbourg and Dagsberg are going to the wars, I will go."

Monsieur Goulden made no remark.

"Every one is free to do as he pleases," said he, after a while; "but I am glad that Joseph thinks as I do."

Then there was silence, and toward two o'clock Aunt Grédel arose and took her basket. She seemed utterly cast down, and said:

"Joseph, you will not listen to me, but no matter. With God's grace, all will yet be well. You will return if He wills it, and Catharine will wait for you."

Catharine wept again, and I more than she; so that Monsieur Goulden himself could not help shedding tears.

At length Catharine and her mother descended the stairs, and Aunt Grédel called out from the bottom:

"Try to come and see us once or twice again, Joseph."

"Yes, yes," I answered, shutting the door.

I could no longer stand. Never had I been so miserable, and even now, when I think of it, my heart chills.

VII.

From that day I could think of nothing but my misfortune. I tried to work, but my thoughts were far away, and Monsieur Goulden said:

"Joseph, stop working. Make the most of the little time you can remain among us; go to see Catharine and Mother Grédel. I still think they will exempt you, but who can tell? They need men so much that it may be a long time coming."

I went every morning then to Quatre-Vents, and passed my days with Catharine. We were very sorrowful, but very glad to see each other. We loved one another even more than before, if that were possible. Catharine sometimes tried to sing as in the good old times; but suddenly she would burst into tears. Then we wept together, and Aunt Grédel would rail at the wars which brought misery to every one. She said that the Council of Revision deserved to be hung; that they were all robbers, banded together to poison our lives. It solaced us a little to hear her talk thus, and we thought she was right.

I returned to the city about eight or nine o'clock in the evening, when they closed the gates, and as I passed, I saw the small inns full of conscripts and old returned soldiers drinking together. The conscripts always paid; the others, with dirty police-caps cocked over their ears, red noses, and horse-hair stocks in place of shirt-collars, twisted their moustaches and related with majestic air their battles, their marches, and their duels. One can imagine nothing viler than those holes, full of smoke, cobwebs hanging on the black beams, those old sworders and young men drinking, shouting, and beating the tables like crazy people; and behind, in the shadow, old Annette Schnaps or Marie Héring—her old wig stuck back on her head, her comb with only three teeth remaining, crosswise, in it—gazing on the scene, or emptying a mug to the health of the braves.

It was sad to see the sons of peasants, honest and laborious fellows, leading such an existence; but no one thought of working, and any one of them would have given his life for two farthings. Worn out with shouting, drinking, and internal grief, they ended by falling asleep over the table, while the old fellows emptied their cups, singing:

"'Tis glory calls us on!"

I saw these things, and I blessed heaven for having given me, in my wretchedness, kind hearts to keep up my courage, and prevent my falling into such hands.

This state of affairs lasted until the twenty-fifth of January. For some days a great number of Italian conscripts—Piedmontese and Genoese—had been arriving in the city; some stout and fat as Savoyards fed upon chestnuts—their cocked hats on their curly heads; their linsey-woolsey pantaloons dyed a dark green, and their short vests also of wool, but brick-red, fastened around their waists by a leather belt. They wore enormous shoes, and ate their cheese seated along the old market-place. Others were dried up, lean, brown, shivering in their long cassocks, seeing nothing but snow upon the roofs and gazing with their large, black, mournful eyes upon the women who passed. They were exercised every day in marching, and were going to fill up the skeleton of the Sixth regiment of the line at Mayence, and were then resting for a while in the infantry barracks.

The captain of the recruits, who was named Vidal, lodged over our room. He was a square-built, solid, very strong-looking man, and was, too, very kind and civil. He came to us to have his watch repaired, and when he learned that I was a conscript and was afraid I should never return, he encouraged me, saying that it was all habit; that at the end of five or six months one fights and marches as he eats his dinner; and that many so accustom themselves to shooting at people that they consider themselves unhappy when they are deprived of that amusement.

But his mode of reasoning was not to my taste; the more so as I saw five or six large grains of powder on one of his cheeks, which had entered deeply, and as he explained to me that they came from a shot which a Russian fired almost under his nose, such a life disgusted me more and more, and as several days had already passed without news, I began to think they had forgotten me, as they did Jacob, of Chèvre

Hof, of whose extraordinary luck every one yet talks. Aunt Grédel herself said to me every time I went there, "Well, well! they will let us alone after all!" When, on the morning of the twenty-fifth of January, as I was about starting for Quatre-Vents, Monsieur Goulden, who was working at his bench with a thoughtful air, turned to me with tears in his eyes and said:

"Listen, Joseph! I wanted to let you have one night more of quiet sleep; but you must know now, my child, that yesterday evening the brigadier of the gendarmes brought me your marching orders. You go with the Piedmontese and Genoese and five or six young men of the city—young Klipfel, young Lœrig, Jean Léger, and Gaspard Zébédé. You go to Mayence."

I felt my knees give way as he spoke, and I sat down unable to speak. Monsieur Goulden took my marching orders, beautifully written, out of a drawer, and began to read them slowly. All that I remember is that Joseph Bertha, native of Dabo, Canton of Phalsbourg, Arrondissement of Sarrebourg, was incorporated in the Sixth regiment of the line, and that he was to join his corps the twenty-ninth of January at Mayence.

This letter produced as bad an effect on me as

if I had know nothing of it before. It seemed something new, and I grew angry.

Monsieur Goulden, after a moment's silence, added:

"The Italians start to day at eleven."

Then, as if awakening from a horrible dream, I cried:

"But shall I not see Catharine again?"

"Yes, Joseph, yes," said he, in a trembling voice. "I notified Mother Grédel and Catharine, and thus, my boy, they will come, and you can embrace them before leaving."

I saw his grief, and it made me sadder yet, so that I had a hard struggle to keep myself from bursting into tears.

He continued after a pause:

"You need not be anxious about anything, Joseph. I have prepared all beforehand; and when you return, if it please God to keep me so long in this world, you will find me always the same. I am beginning to grow old, and my greatest happiness would be to keep you for a son, for I found you good-hearted and honest. I would have given you what I possess, and we would have been happy together. Catharine and you would have been my children. But since it is otherwise, let us be resigned. It is only for a little while. You will be sent back, I am sure. They will soon see that you cannot make long marches."

While he spoke, I sat silently sobbing, my face buried in my hands.

At last he arose and took from a closet a soldier's knapsack of cowskin, which he placed upon the table. I looked at him, thinking of nothing but the pain of parting.

"Here is your knapsack," he added; "and I have put in it all that you require; two linen shirts, two flannel waistcoats, and all the rest. You will receive at Mayence two soldier's shirts, —all that you will need; but I have made for you some shoes, for nothing is worse than those given the soldiers, which are almost always of horse-hide and chafe the feet fearfully. You are none too strong in your leg, my poor boy. Well, well, that is all."

He placed the knapsack upon the table and sat down.

Without, we heard the Italians making ready to depart. Above us Captain Vidal was giving his orders. He had his horse at the barracks of the gendarmerie, and was telling his orderly to see that he was well rubbed and had received his hay.

All this bustle and movement produced a strange effect upon me, and I could not yet realize that I must quit the city. As I was thus in the greatest distress, the door opened and Catharine entered weeping, while Mother Grédel cried out:

"I told you you should have fled to Switzerland; that these rogues would finish by carrying you off. I told you so, and you would not believe me."

"Mother Grédel," replied Monsieur Goulden, "to go to do his duty is not so great an evil as to be despised by honest people. Instead of all these cries and reproaches, which serve no good purpose, you would do better to comfort and encourage Joseph."

"Ah!" said she; "I do not reproach him, although this is terrible."

Catharine did not leave me; she sat by me and we embraced each other, and she said, pressing my arm:

"You will return?"

"Yes, yes," said I, in a low voice. "And you—you will always think of me; you will not love another?"

She answered, sobbing:

"No, no! I will never love any but you."

This lasted a quarter of an hour, when the door opened and Captain Vidal entered, his cloak rolled like a hunting-horn over his shoulder.

"Well," said he, "well; how goes our young man?"

"Here he is," answered Monsieur Goulden.

"Ah!" remarked the captain; "you are making yourself miserable. It is natural. I remember when I departed for the army. We have all a home."

Then, raising his voice, he said:

"Come, come, young man, courage! We are no longer children."

He looked at Catharine.

"I see all," said he to Monsieur Goulden. "I can understand why he does not want to go."

The drums beat in the street and he added:

"We have yet twenty minutes before starting," and, throwing a glance at me, "Do not fail to be at the first call, young man," said he, pressing Monsieur Goulden's hand.

He went out, and we heard his horse pawing at the door.

The morning was overcast, and grief overwhelmed me. I could not leave Catharine.

Suddenly the roll beat. The drums were all collected in the square. Monsieur Goulden, taking the knapsack by its straps, said in a grave voice:

"Joseph, now the last embrace: it is time to go."

I stood up, pale as ashes. He fastened the knapsack to my shoulders. Catharine sat sobbing, her face covered with her apron. Aunt Grédel looked on with lips compressed.

The roll continued for a time, then suddenly ceased.

"The call is about commencing," said Monsieur Goulden, embracing me. Then the fountains of his heart burst forth; tears sprang to his eyes; and calling me his child, his son, he whispered, "Courage!"

Aunt Grédel seated herself again, and as I bent toward her, taking my head between her hands, she sobbed:

"I always loved you, Joseph; ever since you were a baby. You never gave me cause of grief —and now you must go. O God! O God!"

I wept no longer.

When Aunt Grédel released me, I looked a moment at Catharine, who stood motionless. I rushed to her and threw myself on her neck.

She still kept her seat. Then I turned quickly to go, when she cried, in heart-breaking tones:

"O Joseph! Joseph!"

I looked back. We threw ourselves into each other's arms, and for some minutes remained so, sobbing. Her strength seemed to leave her, and I placed her in the arm-chair, and rushed out of the house.

I was already on the square, in the midst of the Italians and of a crowd of people crying for their sons or brothers. I saw nothing; I heard nothing.

When the roll of the drums began again, I looked around, and saw that I was between Klipfel and Furst, all three with our knapsacks on our backs. Their parents stood before us, weeping as if at their funeral. To the right, near the town-hall, Captain Vidal, on his little gray horse, was conversing with two infantry officers. The sergeants called the roll, and we answered. They called Zébédé, Furst, Klipfel, Bertha; we answered like the others. Then the captain gave the word, "March!" and we went, two abreast, toward the French gate.

At the corner of Spitz's bakery, an old woman cried, in a choking voice, from a window:

"Kasper! Kasper!"

It was Zébédé's grandmother. His lips trembled. He waved his hand without replying, and passed on with downcast face.

I shuddered at the thought of passing my home. As we neared it, my knees trembled, and I heard some one call at the window; but I turned my head toward the "Red Ox," and the rattle of the drums drowned the voices.

The children ran after us, shouting:

"There goes Joseph! there goes Klipfel!"

Under the French gate, the men on guard, drawn up in line on each side, gazed on us as we passed at shoulder arms. We passed the outposts, and the drum ceased playing as we turned to the right. Nothing was heard but the plash of footsteps in the mud, for the snow was melting.

We had passed the farm-house of Gerberhoff, and were going to the great bridge, when I heard some one call me. It was the captain, who cried from his horse:

"Very well done, young man; I am satisfied with you."

Hearing this, I could not help again bursting into tears, and the big Furst, too, wept, as we marched along; the others, pale as marble, said nothing. At the bridge, Zébédé took out his pipe to smoke. In front of us, the Italians talked and laughed among themselves; their three weeks of service had accustomed them to this life.

Once on the way to Metting, more than a league from the city, as we began to descend, Klipfel touched me on the shoulder, and whispered:

"Look yonder."

I looked, and saw Phalsbourg far beneath us; the barracks, the magazines, the steeple whence I had seen Catharine's home six weeks before, with old Brainstein—all were in the gray distance, with the woods all around. I would have stopped a few moments, but the squad marched on, and I had to keep pace with them. We entered Metting.

"LOOK YONDER." (Page 108.)

VIII.

THAT same day we went as far as Bitche; the next, to Hornbach; then to Kaiserslautern. It began to snow again.

How often during that long march did I sigh for the thick cloak of Monsieur Goulden, and his double-soled shoes.

We passed through innumerable villages, sometimes on the mountains, sometimes in the plains. As we entered each little town, the drums began to beat, and we marched with heads erect, marking the step, trying to assume the mien of old soldiers. The people looked out of their little windows, or came to the doors, saying, "There go the conscripts!"

At night we halted, glad to rest our weary feet —I, especially. I cannot say that my leg hurt me, but my feet! I had never undergone such fatigue.

With our billet for lodging we had the right to a corner of the fire, but our hosts also gave us a place at the table. We had nearly always buttermilk and potatoes, and often fresh cheese or a dish of sauer-kraut. The children came to look at us, and the old women asked us from what place we came, and what our business was before we left home. The young girls looked sorrowfully at us, thinking of their sweethearts, who had gone five, six, or seven months before. Then they would take us to their son's bed. With what pleasure I stretched out my tired limbs! How I wished to sleep all our twelve hours' halt! But early in the morning, at daybreak, the rattling of the drums awoke me. I gazed at the brown rafters of the ceiling, the window-panes covered with frost, and asked myself where I was. Then my heart would grow cold, as I thought that I was at Bitche—at Kaiserslautern—that I was a conscript; and I had to dress fast as I could, catch up my knapsack, and answer the roll-call.

"A good journey to you!" said the hostess, awakened so early in the morning.

"Thank you," replied the conscript.

And we marched on.

Yes! a good journey to you! They will not

see you again, poor wretch! How many others have followed the same road!

I will never forget how at Kaiserslautern, the second day of our march, having unstrapped my knapsack to take out a white shirt, I discovered, beneath, a little pocket, and opening it I found fifty-four francs in six-livre pieces. On the paper wrapped around them were these words, written by Monsieur Goulden:

"While you are at the wars, be always good and honest. Think of your friends and of those for whom you would be willing to sacrifice your life, and treat the enemy with humanity that they may so treat our soldiers. May heaven guide you, and protect you in your dangers! You will find some money inclosed; for it is a good thing, when far from home and all who love you, to have a little of it. Write to us as often as you can. I embrace you, my child, and press you to my heart."

As I read this, the tears forced themselves to my eyes, and I thought, "Thou art not wholly abandoned, Joseph: fond hearts are yearning towards you. Never forget their kind counsels."

At last, on the fifth day, about ten o'clock in the evening, we entered Mayence. As long as I live I will remember it. It was terribly cold.

We had begun our march at early dawn, and, long before reaching the city, had passed through villages filled with soldiers—calvary, infantry, dragoons in their short jackets—some digging holes in the ice to get water for their horses, others dragging bundles of forage to the doors of the stables; powder-wagons, carts full of cannon-balls, all white with frost, stood on every side; couriers, detachments of artillery, pontoon-trains, were coming and going over the white ground: and no more attention was paid to us than if we were not in existence.

Captain Vidal, to warm himself, had dismounted and marched with us on foot. The officers and sergeants hastened us on. Five or six Italians had fallen behind and remained in the villages, no longer able to advance. My feet were sore and burning, and at the last halt I could scarcely rise to resume the march. The others from Phalsbourg, however, kept bravely on.

Night had fallen; the sky sparkled with stars. Every one gazed forward, and said to his comrade, "We are nearing it! we are nearing it!" for along the horizon a dark line of seeming cloud, glittering here and there with flashing points, told that a great city lay before us.

At last we entered the advanced works, and passed through the zigzag earthen bastions. Then we dressed our ranks and marked the step, as we usually did when approaching a town. At the corner of a sort of demilune we saw the frozen fosse of the city, and the brick ramparts towering above, and opposite us an old, dark gate, with the drawbridge raised. Above stood a sentinel, who, with his musket raised, cried out:

"Who goes there?"

The captain, going forward alone, replied:

"France!"

"What regiment?"

"Recruits for the Sixth of the Line."

A silence ensued. Then the drawbridge was lowered, and the guard turned out and examined us, one of them carrying a great torch. Captain Vidal, a few paces in advance of us, spoke to the commandant of the post, who called out at length:

"Pass when you please."

Our drums began to beat, but the captain ordered them to cease, and we crossed a long bridge and passed through a second gate like the first. Then we were in the streets of the city, which were paved with smooth round stones. Every one tried his best to march steadily; for, although it was night, all the inns and shops along the way were opened and their large windows were shining, and hundreds of people were passing to and fro as if it were broad day.

We turned five or six corners and soon arrived in a little open place before a high barrack, where we were ordered to halt.

There was a shed at the corner of the barrack, and in it a *cantinière* seated behind a small table, under a great tri-colored umbrella from which hung two lanterns.

Several officers came up as soon as we halted; they were the commandant Gémeau and some others whom I have since known. They pressed our captain's hand laughing, then looked at us and ordered the roll to be called. After that, we each received a ration of bread and a billet for lodging. We were told that roll-call would take place the next morning at eight o'clock for the distribution of arms, and then we were ordered to break ranks, while the officers turned up a street to the left and went into a great coffee-house, the entrance of which was approached by a flight of fifteen steps.

But we, with our billets for lodging—what were we to do with them in the middle of such a city, and, above all, the Italians, who did not know a word either of German or French?

My first idea was to see the *cantinière* under her umbrella. She was an old Alsatian, round and chubby, and, when I asked for the *Capougner-Strasse*, she replied:

"What will you pay for?"

I was obliged to take a glass of brandy with her; then she said:

"Look just opposite there; if you turn the first corner to the right, you will find the *Capougner-Strasse*. Good-evening, conscript."

She laughed.

Big Furst and Zébédé were also billeted in the *Capougner-Strasse*, and we set out, glad enough to be able to limp together through the strange city.

Furst found his house first, but it was shut; and while he was knocking at the door, I found mine, which had a light in two windows. I pushed at the door, it opened, and I entered a dark alley, whence came a smell of fresh bread, which was very welcome. Zébédé had to go further on.

I called out in the alley:

"Is any one here?"

Just then an old woman appeared with a candle, at the top of a wooden staircase.

"What do you want?" she asked.

I told her that I was billeted at her house. She came down-stairs, and, looking at my billet, told me in German to follow her.

I ascended the stairs. Passing an open door, I saw two men naked to the waist at work before an oven. I was, then, at a baker's, and her having so much work accounted for the old woman being up so late. She wore a cap with black ribbons, a large blue apron, and her arms were bare to the elbows; she, too, had been working, and seemed very sorrowful. She led me into a good-sized room with a porcelain stove and a bed at the further end.

"You come late," she said.

"We were marching all day," I replied, "and I am fainting with hunger and weariness."

She looked at me and I heard her say:

"Poor child! poor child! Well, take off your shoes and put on these sabots."

Then she made me sit before the stove, and asked:

"Are your feet sore?"

"Yes, they have been so for three days."

She put the candle upon the table and went out. I took off my coat and shoes. My feet were blistered and bleeding, and pained me horribly, and I felt for the moment as if it would almost be better to die at once than continue in such suffering.

This thought had more than once arisen to my mind in the march, but now, before that good fire, I felt so worn, so miserable, that I would gladly have lain myself down to sleep forever, notwithstanding Catharine, Aunt Grédel, and all who loved me. Truly, I needed God's assistance.

While these thoughts were running through my head, the door opened, and a tall, stout man, gray-haired, but yet strong and healthy, entered. He was one of those I had seen at work below, and held in his hands a bottle of wine and two glasses.

"Good-evening!" said he gravely and kindly.

I looked up. The old woman was behind him. She was carrying a little wooden tub, which she placed on the floor near my chair.

"Take a foot-bath," said she; "it will do you good."

This kindness on the part of a stranger, affected me more than I cared to show, and I thought: "There are kind people in the world." I took off my stockings; my feet were bleeding, and the good old dame repeated, as she gazed at them:

"Poor child! poor child!"

The man asked me whence I came. I told him from Phalsbourg in Lorraine. Then he told his wife to bring some bread, adding that, after we had taken a glass of wine together, he would leave me to the repose I needed so much.

He pushed the table before me, as I sat with my feet in the bath, and we each drained a glass of good white wine. The old woman returned with some hot bread, over which she had spread fresh, half-melted butter. Then I knew how hungry I was. I was almost ill. The good people saw my eagerness for food; for the woman said:

"Before eating, my child, you must take your feet out of the bath."

She knelt down and dried my feet with her apron before I knew what she was about to do. I cried:

"Good Heavens! madame; you treat me as if I were your son."

"THERE ARE KIND PEOPLE IN THE WORLD." (Page 120.)

She replied, after a moment's mournful silence:
"We have a son in the army."

Her voice trembled as she spoke, and my heart bled within me. I thought of Catharine and Aunt Grédel, and could not speak again. I ate and drank with a pleasure I never before felt in doing so. The two old people sat gazing kindly on me, and, when I had finished, the man said :

"Yes, we have a son in the army; he went to Russia last year, and we have not since heard from him. These wars are terrible!"

He spoke dreamily, as if to himself, all the while walking up and down the room, his hands crossed behind his back. My eyes began to close when he said suddenly:

"Come, wife. Good night, conscript."

They went out together, she carrying the tub.

"God reward you," I cried, "and bring your son safe home!"

In a minute I was undressed, and, sinking on the bed, I was almost immediately buried in a deep sleep.

IX.

The next morning I awoke at about seven o'clock. A trumpet was sounding the recall at the corner of the street; horses, wagons, and men and women on foot were hurrying past the house. My feet were yet somewhat sore, but nothing to what they had been; and when I had dressed, I felt like a new man, and thought to myself:

"Joseph, if this continues, you will soon be a soldier. It is only the first step that costs."

I dressed in this cheerful mood. The baker's wife had put my shoes to dry before the fire, after filling them with hot ashes to keep them from growing hard. They were well greased and shining.

Then I buckled on my knapsack, and hurried out, without having time to thank those good people—a duty I intended to fulfil after roll-call. At the end of the street—on the square—many of our Italians were already waiting, shivering around the fountain. Furst, Klipfel, and Zébédé arrived a moment after.

Cannon and their caissons covered one entire side of the square. Horses were being brought to water, led by hussars and dragoons. Opposite us were cavalry barracks, high as the church at Phalsbourg, while around the other three sides rose old houses with sculptured gables, like those at Saverne, but much larger. I had never seen anything like all this, and while I stood gazing around, the drums began to beat, and each man took his place in the ranks, and we were informed, first in Italian and then in French, that we were about to receive our arms, and each one was ordered to stand forth as his name was called.

The wagons containing the arms now came up, and the call began. Each received a cartouche-box, a sabre, a bayonet, and a musket. We put them on as well as we could, over our blouses, coats or great-coats, and we looked, with our hats, our caps, and our arms, like a veritable band of banditti. My musket was so long and heavy that I could scarcely carry it; and the Sergeant Pinto showed me how to buckle on the cartouche-box. He was a fine fellow, Pinto.

So many belts crossing my chest made me feel as if I could scarcely breathe, and I saw at once that my miseries had not yet ended.

After the arms, an ammunition-wagon advanced, and they distributed fifty rounds of cartridges to each man. This was no pleasant augury. Then, instead of ordering us to break ranks and return to our lodgings, Captain Vidal drew his sabre and shouted:

"By file right—march!"

The drums began to beat. I was grieved at not being able to thank my hosts for their kindness, and thought that they would consider me ungrateful. But that did not prevent my following the line of march.

We passed through a long winding street, and soon found ourselves without the glacis, and near the frozen Rhine. Across the river high hills appeared, and on the hills, old, gray, ruined castles, like those of Haut-Bas and Géroldseck in the Vosges.

The battalion descended to the river-bank, and crossed upon the ice. The scene was magnificent

—dazzling. We were not alone on the ice; five or six hundred paces before us there was a train of powder wagons guarded by artillerymen on the way to Frankfort. Crossing the river, we continued our march for five hours through the mountains. Sometimes we discovered villages in the defiles; and Zébédé, who was next to me, said:

"As we had to leave home, I would rather go as a soldier than otherwise. At least we shall see something new every day, and, if we are lucky enough ever to return, how much we will have to talk of!"

"Yes," said I; "but I would like better to have less to talk about, and to live quietly, toiling on my own account and not on account of others, who remain safe at home while we climb about here on the ice."

"You do not care for glory," said he; "and yet glory is something."

And I answered him:

"Glory is not for such as we, Zébédé; it is for others who live well, eat well, and sleep well. They have dancings and rejoicings, as we see by the gazettes, and glory too in the bargain, when we have won it by dint of sweat, fasting and broken bones. But poor wretches like us, forced away from home, when at last they return, after losing their habits of labor and industry, and, mayhap a limb, get but little of your glory. Many a one, among their old friends—no better men than they—who were not, perhaps, so good workmen, have made money during the conscript's seven years of war, have opened a shop, married their sweethearts, had pretty children, are men of position—city councillors—notables. And when the others, who have returned from seeking glory by killing their fellow-men, pass by with their chevrons on their arms, those old friends turn a cold shoulder upon them, and if the soldier has a red nose through drinking brandy which was necessary to keep his blood warm in the rain, the snow, the forced march, while they were drinking good wine, they say—'There goes a drunkard!' and the poor conscript, who only asked to be let stay at home and work, becomes a sort of beggar. This is what I think about the matter, Zébédé; I cannot see the justice of all this, and I would rather have these friends of glory go fight themselves, and leave us to remain in peace at home."

"Well," he replied, "I think much as you do;

but, as we are forced to fight, it is as well to say that we are fighting for glory. If we go about looking miserable, people will laugh at us."

Conversing thus, we reached a large river, which, the sergeant told us, was the Main, and near it, upon our road, was a little village. We did not know the name of the village, but there we halted.

We entered the houses, and those who could bought some brandy, wine, and bread. Those who had no money crunched their ration of biscuits, and gazed wistfully at their more fortunate comrades.

About five in the evening we arrived at Frankfort, which is a city yet older than Mayence, and full of Jews. They took us to a place called Saxenhausen, where the Tenth Hussars and the Baden Chasseurs were in barracks,—old buildings which were formerly a hospital, as I was told and believe, for within there was a large yard, with arches under the walls; beneath these arches the horses were stabled, and in the rooms above, the men.

We arrived at this place after passing through innumerable little streets, so narrow that we could scarcely see the stars between the chimneys. Captain Florentin, and the two lieutenants, Clavel and Bretonville, were awaiting us. After roll-call our sergeants led us by detachments to the rooms above the Chasseurs. They were great halls with little windows, and between the windows were the beds.

Sergeant Pinto hung his lantern to the pillar in the middle; each man placed his piece in the rack, and then took off his knapsack, his blouse and his shoes, without speaking. Zébédé was my bed-fellow. God knows we were sleepy enough. Twenty minutes after, we were buried in slumber.

Missing Page

Missing Page

X.

AT Frankfort I learned to understand military life. Up to that time I had been but a simple conscript, then I became a soldier. I do not speak merely of drill,—the way of turning the head right or left, measuring the steps, lifting the hand to the height of the first or second band to load, aiming, recovering arms at the word of command—that is only an affair of a month or two, if a man really desires to learn; but I speak of discipline—of remembering that the corporal is always in the right when he speaks to a private soldier, the sergeant when he speaks to the corporal, the sergeant-major when speaking to the sergeant, the second lieutenant when he orders the sergeant-major, and so on to the Marshal of France—even if the superior asserts that two and two make five, or that the moon shines at midday.

This is very difficult to learn; but there is one

thing that assists you immensely, and that is a sort of placard hung up in every room in the barracks, and which is from time to time read to you. This placard presupposes everything that a soldier might wish to do, as, for instance, to return home, to refuse to serve, to resist his officer, and always ends by speaking of death, or at least five years with a ball and chain.

The day after our arrival at Frankfort I wrote to Monsieur Goulden, to Catharine, and to Aunt Grédel. You may imagine how sadly. It seemed to me, in addressing them, that I was yet at home. I told them of the hardships I had undergone, of the good luck that had happened to me at Mayence, and the courage it required not to drop behind in the march. I told them that I was in good health, for which I thanked God, and that I was even stronger than before I left home, and sent them a thousand remembrances. Our Phalsbourg conscripts, who saw me writing, made me add a few words for each of their families. I wrote also to Mayence, to the good couple of the *Capougner–Strasse*, who had been so kind to me, telling them how I was forced to march without being able to thank them, and asking their forgiveness for so doing.

That day, in the afternoon, we received our uniforms. Dozens of Jews made their appearance and bought our old clothes. I kept only my shoes and stockings. The Italians had great difficulty in making these respectable merchants comprehend their wishes, but the Genoese were as cunning as the Jews, and their bargainings lasted until night. Our corporals received more than one glass of wine; it was policy to make friends of them, for morning and evening they taught us the drill in the snow-covered yard. The *cantinière* Christine was always at her post with a warming-pan under her feet. She took young men of good family into special favor, and the young men of good family were all those who spent their money freely. Poor fools! How many of them parted with their last *sou* in return for her miserable flattery! When that was gone they were mere beggars; but vanity rules all, from the conscripts to the generals.

All this time recruits were constantly arriving from France, and ambulances full of wounded from Poland. What a sight was that before the hospital Saint Esprit on the other side of the river! It was a procession without an end. All these poor wretches were frost-bitten; some had their noses, some their ears frozen, others an arm, others a leg! They were laid in the snow to prevent them from dropping to pieces. Others got out of the carts clinging and holding on, and looked at you like wild beasts, their eyes sunk in their heads, their hair bristling up: the gipsies who sleep in nooks in the woods would have had pity on them; and yet these were the best off, because they escaped from the carnage, while thousands of their comrades had perished in the snow, or on the battle-field. Klipfel, Zébédé, Furst, and I often went to see these poor wretches, and never did we see men so miserably clad. Some wore jackets which once belonged to Cossacks, crushed shakos, women's dresses, and many had only handkerchiefs wound round their feet in lieu of shoes and stockings. They gave us a history of the retreat from Moscow, and then we knew that the twenty-ninth bulletin told only truth.

These stories enraged our men against the Russians. Many said, "If the war would only begin again, they would have a hard job of it then: it is not over! it is not over!" I was at times almost overcome with wrath after hearing some tale of horror; and sometimes I thought to myself, "Joseph, are you not losing your wits? These Russians are defending their families, their homes, all that man holds most dear. We hate them for defending themselves; we would have despised them had they not done so."

But about this time an extraordinary event occurred.

You must know that my comrade, Zébédé, was the son of the gravedigger of Phalsbourg, and sometimes between ourselves we called him "Gravedigger." This he took in good part from us; but one evening after drill, as he was crossing the yard, a hussar cried out:

"Halloo, Gravedigger! help me to drag in these bundles of straw."

Zébédé, turning about, replied:

"My name is not Gravedigger, and you can drag in your own straw. Do you take me for a fool?"

Then the other cried in a still louder tone:

"Conscript, you had better come, or beware!"

Zébédé, with his great hooked nose, his gray eyes and thin lips, never bore too good a character for mildness. He went up to the hussar and asked:

"What is that you say?"

"I tell you to take up those bundles of straw, and quickly, too. Do you hear, conscript?"

He was quite an old man, with moustaches and red, bushy whiskers. Zébédé seized one of the latter, but received two blows in the face. Nevertheless, a fist-full of the whisker remained in his grasp, and, as the dispute had attracted a crowd to the spot, the hussar shook his finger, saying:

"You will hear from me to-morrow, conscript."

"Very good," returned Zébédé; "we shall see. You will probably hear from me too, veteran."

He came immediately after to tell me all this, and I, knowing that he had never handled a weapon more warlike than a pickaxe, could not help trembling for him.

"Listen, Zébédé," I said; "all that there now remains for you to do, since you do not want to desert, is to ask pardon of this old fellow; for those veterans all know some fearful tricks of fence which they have brought from Egypt or Spain, or somewhere else. If you wish, I will lend you a crown to pay for a bottle of wine to make up the quarrel."

But he, knitting his brows, would hear none of this.

"Rather than beg his pardon," said he, "I would go and hang myself. I laugh him and his comrades to scorn. If he has tricks of fence,

I have a long arm, that will drive my sabre through his bones as easily as his will penetrate my flesh."

The thought of the blows made him insensible to reason; and soon Chazy, the *maître d'armes*, Corporal Fleury, Furst, and Leger came in. They all said that Zébédé was in the right, and the *maître d'armes* added that blood alone could wash out the stain of a blow; that the honor of the recruits required Zebede to fight.

Zébédé answered proudly that the men of Phalsbourg had never feared the sight of a little blood, and that he was ready. Then the *maître d'armes* went to see our Captain, Florentin, who was one of the most magnificent men imaginable — tall, well-formed, broad-shouldered, with regular features, and the Cross, which the Emperor had himself given him at Eylau. The captain even went further than the *maître d'armes*; he thought it would set the conscripts a good example, and that if Zébédé refused to fight he would be unworthy to remain in the Third Battalion of the Sixth of the Line.

All that night I could not close my eyes. I heard the deep breathing of my poor comrade as he slept, and I thought: "Poor Zébédé! another day, and you will breathe no more." I shuddered to think how near I was to a man so near death. At last, as day broke, I fell asleep, when suddenly I felt a cold blast of wind strike me. I opened my eyes, and there I saw the old hussar. He had lifted up the coverlet of our bed, and said as I awoke:

"Up, sluggard! I will show you what manner of man you struck."

Zébédé rose tranquilly, saying:

"I was asleep, veteran; I was asleep."

The other, hearing himself thus mockingly called "veteran," would have fallen upon my comrade in his bed; but two tall fellows who served him as seconds held him back, and, besides, the Phalsbourg men were there.

"Quick, quick! Hurry!" cried the old hussar.

But Zébédé dressed himself calmly, without any haste. After a moment's silence, he said:

"Have we permission to go outside our quarters, old fellows?"

"There is room enough for us in the yard," replied one of the hussars.

Zébédé put on his great-coat, and, turning to me, said:

"Joseph and you, Klipfel, I choose for my seconds."

But I shook my head.

"Well, then, Furst," said he.

The whole party descended the stairs together. I thought Zébédé was lost, and thought it hard, that not only must the Russians seek our lives, but that we must seek each other's.

All the men in the room crowded to the windows. I alone remained behind upon my bed. At the end of five minutes the clash of sabres made my heart almost cease to beat; the blood seemed no longer to flow through my veins.

But this did not last long; for suddenly Klipfel exclaimed, "Touched!"

Then I made my way—I know not how—to a window, and, looking over the heads of the others, saw the old hussar leaning against the wall, and Zébédé rising, his sabre all dripping with blood. He had fallen upon his knees during the fight, and, while the old man's sword pierced the air just above his shoulder, he plunged his blade into the hussar's breast. If he had not slipped, he himself would have been run through and through.

The hussar sank at the foot of the wall. His seconds lifted him in their arms, while Zébédé pale as a corpse, gazed at his bloody sabre, and

Klipfel handed him his cloak. Almost immediately the reveille was sounded, and we went off to morning call.

These events happened on the eighteenth of February. The same day we received orders to pack our knapsacks, and left Frankfort for Seligenstadt, where we remained until the eighth of March, by which time all the recruits were well instructed in the use of the musket and the school of the platoon. From Seligenstadt we went to Schweinheim, and on the twenty-fourth of March, 1813, joined the division at Aschaffenbourg, where Marshal Ney passed us in review.

The captain of the company was named Florentin; the lieutenant, Bretonville; the commandant of the battalion, Gémeau; the captain, Vidal; the colonel, Zapfel; the general of brigade, Ladoucette; and the general of division, Souham. These are things that every soldier should know.

XI.

The melting of the snows began about the middle of March. I remember that during the great review of Aschaffenbourg, on a large open space whence one saw the Main as far as eye could reach, the rain never ceased to fall from ten o'clock in the morning till three o'clock in the afternoon. We had on our left a castle, from the windows of which people looked out quite at their ease, while the water ran into our shoes. On the right the river rushed, foaming, seen dimly as if through a mist. Every moment, to keep us brightened up, the order rang out:

"Carry arms! Shoulder arms!"

The Marshal advanced slowly, surrounded by his staff. What consoled Zébédé was, that we were about to see "the bravest of the brave." I thought "If I could only get a place at the corner of a good fire, I would gladly forego that pleasure."

At last he arrived in front of us, and I can yet see him, his chapeau dripping with rain; his blue coat covered with embroidery and decorations, and his great boots. He was a handsome, florid man, with a short nose and sparkling eyes. He did not seem at all haughty; for, as he passed our company, who presented arms, he turned suddenly in his saddle and said:

"Hold! It is Florentin!"

Then the captain stood erect, not knowing what to reply. It seemed that the Marshal and he had been common soldiers together in the time of the Republic. The captain at last answered:

"Yes, Marshal; it is Sebastian Florentin."

"Faith, Florentin," said the Marshal, stretching his arm toward Russia, "I am glad to see you again. I thought we had left you there."

All our company felt honored, and Zébédé said:

"That is what I call a man. I would spill my blood for him."

I could not see why Zébédé should wish to spill his blood because the Marshal had spoken a few words to an old comrade.

That's all I remember of Aschaffenbourg.

In the evening we went in again to eat our soup at Schweinheim, a place rich in wines, hemp, and corn, where almost everybody looked at us with unfriendly eyes.

We lodged by threes or fours in the houses, like so many bailiff's men, and had meat every day, either beef, mutton, or bacon.

Our bread was very good, as was also our wine. But many of our men pretended to find fault with everything, thinking thus to pass for people of consequence. They were mistaken; for more than once I heard the citizens say in German:

"Those fellows, in their own country, were only beggars. If they returned to France, they would find nothing but potatoes to live upon."

And the citizens were quite right; and I always found that people so difficult to please abroad were but poor wretches at home. For my part, I was well content to meet such good fare. Two conscripts from St.-Dié were with me at the village-postmaster's: his horses had almost all been taken for our cavalry. This could not have put him into a good humor; but he said nothing, and smoked his pipe behind the stove from morning till night. His wife was a tall strong woman, and his two daughters were very pretty; they were afraid of us, and ran away when we returned from drill, or from mounting guard at the end of the village.

On the evening of the fourth day, as we were finishing our supper, an old man in great-coat came in. His hair was white, and his mien and appearance neat and respectable. He saluted us, and then said to the master of the house, in German:

"These are recruits?"

"Yes, Monsieur Stenger," replied the other; "we will never be rid of them. If I could poison them all, it would be a good deed."

I turned quietly, and said:

"I understand German: do not speak in such a manner."

The postmaster's pipe fell from his hand

"You are very imprudent in your speech, Monsieur Kalkreuth," said the old man; "if others beside this young man had understood you, you know what would happen."

"It is only my way of talking," replied the postmaster. "What can you expect? When everything is taken from you—when you are robbed, year after year—it is but natural that you should at last speak bitterly."

The old man, who was none other than the pastor of Schweinheim, then said to me:

"Monsieur, your manner of acting is that of an honest man; believe me that Monsieur Kalkreuth is incapable of such a deed—of doing evil even to our enemies."

"I do believe it, sir," I replied, "or I should not eat so heartily of these sausages."

The postmaster, hearing these words, began to laugh, and, in the excess of his joy, cried:

"I would never have thought that a Frenchman could have made me laugh."

My two comrades were ordered for guard duty; they went, but I alone remained. Then the postmaster went after a bottle of old wine, and seated himself at the table to drink with me, which I gladly agreed to. From that day until our departure, these people had every confidence in me. Every evening we chatted at the corner of the fire; the pastor came, and even the young girls would come down stairs to listen. They were of fair and light complexion, with blue eyes; one was perhaps eighteen, the other twenty; I thought I saw in them a resemblance to Catharine, and this made my heart beat.

They knew that I had a sweetheart at home,

because I could not help telling them so, and this made them pity me.

The postmaster complained bitterly of the French; the pastor said they were a vain, immoral nation; and that on that account all Germany would soon rise against us; that they were weary of the evil doings of our soldiers and the cupidity of our generals, and had formed the *Tugend-Bund** to oppose us.

"At first," said he, "you talked to us of liberty: we liked to hear that, and our good wishes were rather for your armies than those of the King of Prussia and Emperor of Austria; you made war upon our soldiers and not upon us; you upheld ideas which every one thought great and just, and so you did not quarrel with peoples but only with their masters. To-day it is very different; all Germany is flying to arms; all her youth are rising, and it is we who talk of Liberty, of Virtue and of Justice to France. He who has them on his side is ever the stronger, because he has against him only the evil-minded of all nations, and has with him youth, courage, great ideas,—everything which lifts the soul above

---

* League of virtue.

thoughts of self, and which urges man to sacrifice his life without regret. You have long had all this, but you wanted it no longer. Long ago, I well remember, your generals fought for Liberty, slept on straw, in barns, like simple soldiers: they were men of might and terror; now they must have their sofas; they are more noble than our nobles and richer than our bankers. So it comes to pass that war, once so grand— once an art, a sacrifice—once devotion to one's country—has become a trade, for sale at more than one market. It is, to be sure, very noble yet, since epaulettes are yet worn, but there is a difference between fighting for immortal ideas and fighting merely to enrich one's self.

"It is now our turn to talk of Liberty and Country; and this is the reason why I think this war will be a sorrowful one for you. All thinking men, from simple students to professors of theology, are rising against you in arms. You have the greatest general of the world at your head, but we have eternal justice. You believe you have the Saxons, the Bavarians, the Badeners and the Hessians on your side; un-deceive yourselves; the children of old Germany well know that the greatest crime, the greatest shame, is to fight against our brothers. Let kings make alliances; the people are against you in spite of them; they are defending their lives, their Fatherland—all that God makes us love and that we cannot betray without crime. All are ready to assail you; the Austrians would massacre you if they could, notwithstanding the marriage of Marie Louise with your Emperor; men begin to see that the interests of Kings are not the interests of all mankind, and that the greatest genius cannot change the nature of things."

Thus would the pastor discourse gravely; but I did not then fully understand what he meant, and I thought, "Words are only words; and bullets are bullets. If we only encounter students and professors of theology, all will go well, and discipline will keep the Hessians and Bavarians and Saxons from turning against us, as it forces us Frenchmen to fight, little as we may like it. Does not the soldier obey the corporal, the corporal the sergeant, and so on to the marshal, who does what the King wishes? One can see very well that this pastor never served in a regiment, for if he did he would know that ideas are nothing and orders everything; but I do not care to contradict him, for then the postmaster would bring me no more wine after supper. Let them think as they please. All that I hope is that we shall have only theologians to fight."

While we used to chat thus, suddenly, on the morning of the twenty-seventh of March, the order for our departure came. The battalion rested that night at Lauterbach, the next at Neukirchen, and we did nothing but march, march, march. Those who did not grow accustomed to carrying the knapsack could not complain of want of practice. How we travelled! I no longer sweated under my fifty cartridges in my cartouche-box, my knapsack on my back and my musket on my shoulder, and I do not know if I limped.

We were not the only ones in motion; all were marching.; everywhere we met regiments on the road, detachments of cavalry, long lines of cannon, ammunition trains—all advancing towards Erfurt, as after a heavy rain thousands of streams, by thousands of channels, seek the river.

Our sergeants keep repeating. "We are nearing them! there will be hot work soon;" and we thought, "So much the better!" that those beggarly Prussians and Russians had drawn their fate upon themselves. If they had remained quiet, we would have been yet in France.

These thoughts embittered us all towards the enemy, and as we met everywhere people who seemed to rejoice alone in fighting, Klipfel and Zébédé talked only of the pleasure it would give them to meet the Prussians; and I, not to seem less courageous than they, adopted the same strain.

On the eighth of April, the battalion entered Erfurt, and I will never forget how, when we broke ranks before the barracks, a package of letters was handed to the sergeant of the company. Among the number was one for me, and I recognized Catharine's writing at once. This affected me so that it made my knees tremble. Zébédé took my musket, telling me to read it, for he, too, was glad to hear from home.

I put it in my pocket, and all our Phalsbourg men followed me to hear it, but I only commenced when I was quietly seated on my bed in the barracks, while they crowded around. Tears rolled down my cheeks as she told me how she remembered and prayed for the far-off conscript.

My comrades, as I read, exclaimed:

"And we are sure that there are some at home to pray for us, too."

One spoke of his mother, another of his sisters, and another of his sweetheart.

At the end of the letter, Monsieur Goulden added a few words, telling me that all our friends were well, and that I should take courage, for our troubles could not last forever. He charged me to be sure to tell my comrades that their friends thought of them and complained of not having received a word from them.

This letter was a consolation to us all. We knew that before many days passed we must be on the field of battle, and it seemed a last farewell from home for at least half of us. Many were never to hear again from their parents, friends, or those who loved them in this world.

XII.

But, as Sergeant Pinto said, all we had yet seen was but the prelude to the ball; the dance was now about to commence.

Meanwhile we did duty at the citadel with a battalion of the Twenty-seventh, and from the top of the ramparts we saw all the environs covered with troops, some bivouacking, others quartered in the villages.

The sergeant had formed a particular friendship for me, and on the eighteenth, on relieving guard at Warthau gate, he said:

"Fusilier Bertha, the Emperor has arrived."

I had yet heard nothing of this, and replied, respectfully:

"I have just had a little glass with the sapper Merlin, sergeant, who was on duty last night at the general's quarters, and he said nothing of it."

Then he, closing his eye, said, with a peculiar expression :

"Everything is moving; I feel his presence in the air. You do not yet understand this, conscript, but he is here; everything says so. Before he came, we were lame, crippled; only a wing of the army seemed able to move at once. But now, look there, see those couriers galloping over the road; all is life. The dance is beginning : the dance is beginning! Kaiserliks and the Cossacks do not need spectacles to see that he is with us; they will feel him presently."

And the sergeant's laugh rang hoarsely from beneath his long moustaches. I had a presentiment that great misfortunes might be coming upon me, yet I was forced to put a good face upon it. But the sergeant was right, for that very day, about three in the afternoon, all the troops stationed around the city were in motion, and at five we were put under arms. The Marshal Prince of Moskowa entered the town surrounded by the officers and generals who composed his staff, and, almost immediately after, the gray-haired Souham followed and passed us in review upon the square. Then he spoke in a loud, clear voice so that every one could hear:

"Soldiers!" said he, "you will form part of the advance-guard of the Third corps. Try to remember that you are Frenchmen. *Vive l'Empereur!*"

All shouted "*Vive l'Empereur!*" till the echoes rang again, while the general departed with Colonel Zapfel.

That night we were relieved by the Hessians, and left Erfurt with the Tenth hussars and a regiment of chasseurs. At six or seven in the morning we were before the city of Weimar, and saw the sun rising on its gardens, its churches, and its houses, as well as on an old castle to the right. Here we bivouacked, and the hussars went forward to reconnoitre the town. About nine, while we were breakfasting, suddenly we heard the rattle of musketry and carbines. Our hussars had encountered the Prussian hussars in the streets, and they were firing on each other. But it was so far off that we saw nothing of the combat.

At the end of an hour the hussars returned, having lost two men. Thus began the campaign.

We remained five days in our camp, while the whole Third corps were coming up. As we were the advance-guard, we started again by way of

Sulza and Warthau. Then we saw the enemy; Cossacks who kept ever beyond the range of our guns, and the further they retired the greater grew our courage.

But it annoyed me to hear Zébédé constantly exclaiming in a tone of ill-humor:

"Will they never stop; never make a stand!"

I thought that if they kept retreating we could ask nothing better. We would gain all we wanted without loss of life or suffering.

But at last they halted on the further side of the broad and deep river, and I saw a great number posted near the bank to cut us to pieces if we should cross unsupported.

It was the twenty-ninth of April, and growing late. Never did I see a more glorious sunset. On the opposite side of the river stretched a wide plain as far as the eye could reach, and on this, sharply outlined against the glowing sky, stood horsemen, with their shakos drooping forward, their green jackets, little cartridge-boxes slung under the arm, and their sky-blue trousers; behind them glittered thousands of lances, and Sergeant Pinto recognized them as the Russian cavalry and Cossacks. He knew the river, too, which, he said was the Saale.

We went as near as we could to the water to exchange shots with the horsemen, but they retired and at last disappeared entirely under the blood-red sky. We made our bivouac along the river, and posted our sentries. On our left was a large village; a detachment was sent to it to purchase meat; for since the arrival of the Emperor we had orders to pay for everything.

During the night other regiments of the division came up; they, too, bivouacked along the bank, and their long lines of fires, reflected in the ever-moving waters, glared grandly through the darkness.

No one felt inclined to sleep. Zébédé, Klipfel, Furst, and I messed together, and we chatted as we lay around our fire:

"To-morrow we will have it hot enough, if we attempt to cross the river! Our friends in Phalsbourg, over their warm suppers, scarcely think of us lying here, with nothing but a piece of cow-beef to eat, a river flowing beside us, the damp earth beneath, and only the sky for a roof, without speaking of the sabre-cuts and bayonet-thrusts our friends yonder have in store for us."

"Bah!" said Klipfel; "this is life. I would not pass my days otherwise. To enjoy life we must be well to-day, sick to-morrow; then we appreciate the pleasure of the change from pain to ease. As for shots and sabre-strokes, with God's aid, we will give as good as we take!"

"Yes," said Zébédé, lighting his pipe, "when I lose my place in the ranks, it will not be for the want of striking hard at the Russians!"

So we lay wakeful for two or three hours. Leger lay stretched out in his great coat, his feet to the fire, asleep, when the sentinel cried:

"Who goes there?"

"France!"

"What regiment?"

"Sixth of the Line."

It was Marshal Ney and General Brenier, with engineer and artillery officers, and guns. The marshal replied "Sixth of the Line," because he knew beforehand that we were there, and this little fact rejoiced us and made us feel very proud. We saw him pass on horseback with General Souham and five or six other officers of high grade, and although it was night we could see them distinctly, for the sky was covered with stars and the moon shone bright; it was almost as light as day.

They stopped at a bend of the river and posted

six guns, and immediately after a pontoon train arrived with oak planks and all things necessary for throwing two bridges across. Our hussars scoured the banks collecting boats, and the artillerymen stood at their pieces to sweep down any who might try to hinder the work. For a long while we watched their labor, while again and again we heard the sentry's "*Qui vive!*" It was the regiments of the Third corps arriving.

At daybreak I fell asleep, and Klipfel had to shake me to arouse me. On every side they were beating the reveille; the bridges were finished, and we were going to cross the Saale.

A heavy dew had fallen, and each man hastened to wipe his musket, to roll up his great coat and buckle it on his knapsack. One assisted the other, and we were soon in the ranks. It might have been four o'clock in the morning, and everything seemed grey in the mist that arose from the river. Already two battalions were crossing on the bridges, the officers and colors in the centre. Then the artillery and caissons crossed.

Captain Florentin had just ordered us to renew our primings, when General Souham, General Chemineau, Colonel Zapfel, and our commandant arrived. The battalion began its march. I looked forward expecting to see the Russians coming on at a gallop, but nothing stirred.

As each regiment reached the further bank it formed square with ordered arms. At five o'clock the entire division had passed. The sun dispersed the mist, and we saw, about three fourths of a league to our right, an old city with its pointed roofs, slated clock-tower, surmounted by a cross, and, further away, a castle; it was Weissenfels.

Between us and the city was a deep valley. Marshal Ney, who had just come up, wished to reconnoitre this before advancing into it. Two companies of the Twenty-seventh were deployed as skirmishers and the squares moved onward in common time, with the officers, sappers, and drums in the centre, the cannon in the intervals and the caissons in the rear.

We all mistrusted this valley—the more so since we had seen, the evening before, a mass of cavalry, which could not have retired beyond the great plain that lay before us. Notwithstanding our distrust, it made us feel very proud and brave to see ourselves drawn up in our long ranks— our muskets loaded, the colors advanced, the generals in the rear full of confidence—to see our masses thus moving onward without hurry, but calmly marking the step ; yes, it was enough to make our hearts beat high with pride and hope! And I said to myself: "Perhaps at sight of us the enemy will fly, which will be the best for them and for us."

I was in the second rank, behind Zébédé, and from time to time I glanced at the other square, which was moving on the same line with us, in the centre of which I saw the marshal and his staff, all trying to catch a glimpse of what was going on ahead.

The skirmishers had by this time reached the ravine, which was bordered with brambles and hedges. I had already seen a movement on its farther side, like the motion of a cornfield in the wind, and the thought struck me that the Russians, with their lances and sabres, were there, although I could scarcely believe it. But when our skirmishers reached the hedges, the fusilade began, and I saw clearly the glitter of their lances. At the same instant a flash like lightning gleamed in front of us, followed by a fierce report. The Russians had their cannon with them ; they had opened on us. I know not what noise made me turn my head, and there I saw an empty space in the ranks to my left.

At the same time Colonel Zapfel said quietly:
"Close up the ranks!"

And Captain Florentin repeated:

"Close up the ranks!"

All this was done so quickly that I had no time for thought. But fifty paces further on another flash shone out; there was another murmur in the ranks—as if a fierce wind was passing—and another vacant space, this time to the right.

And thus, after every shot from the Russians, the colonel said, "Close up the ranks!" and I knew that each time he spoke there was a breach in the living wall! It was no pleasant thing to think of, but still we marched on toward the valley. At last I did not dare to think at all, when General Chemineau, who had entered our square, cried in a terrible voice:

"Halt!"

I looked forward, and saw a mass of Russians coming down upon us.

"Front rank, kneel! Fix bayonets! Ready!" cried the general.

As Zébédé knelt, I was now, so to speak, in the front rank. On came the line of horses, each rider bending over his saddle-bow, with sabre flashing in his hand. Then again the general's voice was heard behind us, calm, tranquil, giving orders as coolly as on parade :

"Attention for the command of fire! Aim! Fire!"

The four squares fired together; it seemed as if the skies were falling in the crash. When the smoke lifted, we saw the Russians broken and flying; but our artillery opened, and the cannon-balls sped faster than they.

"Charge!" shouted the general.

Never in my life did such a wild joy possess me. On every side the cry of *Vive l'Empereur!* shook the air, and in my excitement I shouted like the others. But we could not pursue them far, and soon we were again moving calmly on. We thought the fight was ended; but when within two or three hundred paces of the ravine, we heard the rush of horses, and again the general cried :

"Halt! Kneel! Fix bayonets!"

On came the Russians from the valley like a whirlwind; the earth shook beneath their weight; we heard no more orders, but each man knew that he must fire into the mass, and the file-firing began, rattling like the drums in a grand review. Those who have not seen a battle can form but little idea of the excitement, the confusion, and yet the order of such a moment. A few of the Russians neared us; we saw their forms appear a moment through the smoke, and then saw them no more. In a few moments more the ringing voice of General Chemineau arose, sounding above the crash and rattle:

"Cease firing!"

We scarcely dared obey. Each one hastened to deliver a final shot; then the smoke slowly lifted, and we saw a mass of cavalry ascending the further side of the ravine.

The squares deployed at once into columns; the drums beat the charge; our artillery still continued its fire; we rushed on, shouting:

"Forward! forward! *Vive l'Empereur!*"

We descended the ravine, over heaps of horses and Russians; some dead, some writhing upon the earth, and we ascended the slope toward Weissenfels at a quick step. The Cossacks and chasseurs bent forward in their saddles, their cartridge-boxes dangling behind them, galloping before us in full flight. The battle was won.

But as we reached the gardens of the city, they posted their cannon, which they had brought off with them, behind a sort of orchard, and reopened upon us, a ball carrying away both the axe and head of the sapper, Merlin. The corporal of sappers, Thomé, had his arm fractured by a piece of the axe, and they were compelled to amputate his arm at Weissenfels. Then we started toward them on a run, for the sooner we reached them the less time they would have for firing.

We entered the city at three places, marching through hedges, gardens, hop-fields, and climbing over walls. The marshals and generals followed after. Our regiment entered by an avenue bordered with poplars, which ran along the cemetery, and, as we debouched in the public square another column came through the main street.

There we halted, and the marshal, without losing a moment, dispatched the Twenty-seventh to take a bridge and cut off the enemy's retreat. During this time the rest of the division arrived, and was drawn up in the square. The burgomaster and councillors of Weissenfels were already on the steps of the town-hall to bid us welcome.

When we were re-formed, the Marshal-Prince of Moskowa passed before the front of our battalion and said joyfully:

"Well done! I am satisfied with you! The Emperor will know of your conduct!"

He could not help laughing at the way we rushed on the guns. General Souham cried:

"Things go bravely on!"

He replied:

"Yes, yes; 'tis in the blood! 'tis in the blood:"

The battalion remained there until the next day. We were lodged with the citizens, who were afraid of us and gave us all we asked. The Twenty-seventh returned in the evening and was quartered in the old château. We were very tired. After smoking two or three pipes together, chatting about our glory, Zébédé, Klipfel and I went together to the shop of a joiner and slept on a heap of shavings, and remained there until midnight, when they beat the reveille. We rose; the joiner gave us some brandy, and we went out. The rain was falling in torrents. That night the battalion went to bivouac before the village of Clépen, two hours march from Weissenfels.

Other detachments came and rejoined us. The Emperor had arrived at Weissenfels, and all the third corps were to follow us. We talked only of this all the day; but the day after, at five in the morning, we set off again in the advance.

Before us rolled a river called the Rippach. Instead of turning aside to take the bridge, we forded it where we were. The water reached our waists; and I thought, as I pulled my shoes out of the mud, "If any one had told me this in the days when I was afraid of catching a cold in the head at M. Goulden's, and when I changed my stockings twice a week, I should never have believed it. Well, strange things happen to one in this life."

As we passed down the other bank of the river in the rushes, we discovered a band of Cossacks observing us from the heights to the left. They followed slowly, without daring to attack us, and so we kept on until it was broad day, when suddenly a terrific fusilade and the thunder of heavy guns made us turn our heads toward Clépen. The commandant, on horseback, looked over the tops of the reeds.

The sounds of conflict lasted a considerable time, and Sergeant Pinto said:

"The division is advancing; it is attacked."

The Cossacks gazed, too, toward the fight, and at the end of an hour disappeared. Then we saw the division advancing in column in the plain to the right, driving before them the masses of Russian cavalry.

"Forward!" cried the commandant.

We ran, without knowing why, along the river bank, until we reached an old bridge where the Rippach and Gruna met. Here we were to intercept the enemy: but the Cossacks had discovered our design, and their whole army fell back behind the Gruna, which they forded, and, the division rejoining us, we learned that Marshal Bessières had been killed by a cannon-ball.

We left the bridge to bivouac before the village of Gorschen. The rumor that a great battle was approaching ran through the ranks, and they said that all that had passed was only a trial to see how the recruits would act under fire. One may imagine the reflections of a thoughtful man under such circumstances, among such hare-brained fellows as Furst, Zébédé, and Klipfel, who seemed to rejoice at the prospect, as if it could bring them aught else than bullet-wounds or sabre-cuts. All night long I thought of Catharine, and prayed God to preserve my life and my hands, which are so needful for poor people to gain their bread.

XIII.

WE lighted our fires on the hill before Gross-Gorschen and a detachment descended to the village and brought back five or six old cows to make soup of. But we were so worn out that many would rather sleep than eat. Other regiments arrived with cannon and munitions. About eleven o'clock there were from ten to twelve thousand men there and two thousand and more in the village—all Souham's division. The general and his ordnance officers were quartered in an old mill to the left, near a stream called Floss-Graben. The line of sentries were stretched along the base of the hill a musket-shot off.

At length I fell asleep, but I awoke every hour, and behind us, toward the road leading from the old bridge of Poserna to Lutzen and Leipzig, I heard the rolling of wagons, of artillery and caissons, rising and falling through the silence.

Sergeant Pinto did not sleep; he sat smoking his pipe and drying his feet at the fire. Every time one of us moved, he would try to talk and say:

"Well, conscript?"

But they pretended not to hear him, and turned over, gaping, to sleep again.

The clock of Gross-Gorshen was striking six when I awoke. I was sore and weary yet. Nevertheless, I sat up and tried to warm myself, for I was very cold. The fires were smoking, and almost extinguished. Nothing of them remained but the ashes and a few embers. The sergeant, erect, was gazing over the vast plain where the sun shot a few long lines of gold, and, seeing me awake, put a coal in his pipe and said:

"Well, fusilier Bertha, we are now in the rear-guard."

I did not know what he meant.

"That astonishes you," he continued; "but we have not stirred, while the army has made a half-wheel. Yesterday it was before us in the Rippach; now it is behind us, near Lutzen; and, instead of being in the front we are in rear; so that now," said he, closing an eye and drawing two long puffs of his pipe, "we are the last, instead of the foremost."

"And what do we gain by it?" I asked.

"We gain the honor of first reaching Leipzig, and falling on the Prussians," he replied. "You will understand this by and by, conscript."

I stood up, and looked around. I saw before us a wide, marshy plain, traversed by the Gruna-Bach and the Floss-Graben. A few hills arose along these streams, and beyond ran a large river, which the sergeant told me was the Elster. The morning mist hung over all.

Turning around, I saw behind us in the valley the point of the clock-tower of Gross-Gorschen, and further on, to the right and left, five or six little villages built in the hollows between the hills, for it is a country of hills, and the villages of Kaya, Eisdorf, Starsiedel, Rahna, Klein-Gorschen and Gross-Gorschen, which I knew before, are between them, on the borders of little lakes, where poplars, willows and aspens grow. Gross-Gorschen, where we bivouacked, was furthest advanced in the plain, toward the Elster; Kaya was furthest off, and behind it passed the high-road from Lutzen to Leipzig.

We saw no fires on the hills save those of our division; but the entire corps occupied the villages scattered in our rear, and headquarters were at Kaya.

At seven o'clock the drums and the trumpets of the artillery sounded the reveille. We went down to the village, some to look for wood, others for straw or hay. Ammunition-wagons came up, and bread and cartridges were distributed. There we were to remain, to let the army march by upon Leipzig; this was why Sergeant Pinto said we would be in the rear-guard.

Two *cantinières* arrived from the village; and, as I had yet a few crowns remaining, I offered Klipfel and Zébédé a glass of brandy each, to counteract the effects of the fogs of the night. I also presumed to offer one to Sergeant Pinto, who accepted it, saying that bread and brandy warmed the heart.

We felt quite happy, and no one suspected the horrors the day was to bring forth. We thought the Russians and the Prussians were seeking us behind the Gruna-Bach; but they knew well where we were. And suddenly, about ten o'clock, General Souham, mounted, arrived with his officers. I was sentry near the stacks of arms, and I think I can now see him, as he rode to the top of the hill, with his gray hair and white-bordered hat; and as he took out his field-glass, and, after an earnest gaze, returned quickly, and ordered the drums to beat the recall. The sentries at once fell into the ranks, and Zébédé, who had the eyes of a falcon, said:

"I see yonder, near the Elster, masses of men forming and advancing in good order, and others coming from the marshes by the three bridges. We are lost if all those fall upon our rear!"

"A battle is beginning," said Sergeant Pinto, shading his eyes with his hands, "or I know nothing of war. Those beggarly Prussians and Russians want to take us on the flank with their whole force, as we defile on Leipzig, so as to cut us in two. It is well thought of on their part. We are always teaching them the art of war."

"But what will we do?" asked Klipfel.

"Our part is simple," answered the sergeant. "We are here twelve to fifteen thousand men, with old Souham, who never gave an enemy an inch. We will stand here like a wall, one to six or seven, until the Emperor is informed how matters stand, and sends us aid. There go the staff officers now."

It was true; five or six officers were galloping over the plain of Lutzen toward Leipzig. They sped like the wind, and I prayed to God to have them reach the Emperor in time to send the whole army to our assistance; for there was something horrible in the certainty that we were about to perish, and I would not wish my greatest enemy in such a position as ours was then.

Sergeant Pinto continued:

"You will have a chance now, conscripts; and if any of you come out alive, they will have something to boast of. Look at those blue lines advancing, with their muskets on their shoulders, along Floss-Graben. Each of those lines is a regiment. There are thirty of them. That makes sixty thousand Prussians, without counting those lines of horsemen, each of which is a squadron. Those advancing to their left, near Rippach, glittering in the sun, are the dragoons and cuirassiers of the Russian Imperial Guard. There are eighteen or twenty thousand of them, and I first saw them at Austerlitz, where we fixed them finely. Those masses of lances in the rear are Cossacks. We will have a hundred thousand men on our hands in an hour. This is a fight to win the cross in, and if one does not get it now he can never hope to do so!"

"Do you think so, sergeant?" said Zébédé, whose ideas were never very clear, and who already imagined he held the cross in his fingers, while his eyes glittered with excitement.

"It will be hand to hand," replied the sergeant; "and suppose that in the *melée*, you see a colonel or a flag near you, spring on him or it; never mind sabres or bayonets; seize them, and then your name goes on the list."

As he spoke, I remembered that the Mayor of Phalsbourg had received the cross for having gone to meet the Empress Marie Louise in carriages garlanded with flowers, singing old songs, and I thought his method much preferable to that of Sergeant Pinto.

But I had not time to think more, for the drums beat on all sides, and each one ran to where the arms of his company were stacked and seized his musket. Our officers formed us, great guns came at a gallop from the village, and were posted on the brow of the hill a little to the rear, so that the slope served them as a species of redoubt. Further away, in the villages of Rahna, of Kaya, and of Klein-Gorschen, all was motion, but we were the first the Prussians would fall upon.

The enemy halted about twice a cannon-shot off, and the cavalry swarmed by hundreds up the hill to reconnoitre us. I was in utter despair as I gazed on their immense masses swarming on both sides of the river, the advanced lines of which were already beginning to form in columns, and I said to myself, "This time, Joseph, all is over, all is lost; there is no help for it; all you can do is to revenge yourself, defend yourself, to fight pitilessly, and die."

While these thoughts were passing through my head, General Chemineau galloped along our front, crying :

"Form square."

The officers on the right, on the left, in advance, in the rear, took up the word and it passed from right to left; four squares of four battalions each were formed. I found myself in the third, on one of the interior sides, a circumstance which in some degree reassured me; for I thought that the Prussians, who were advancing in three columns, would first attack those directly opposite them. But scarcely had the thought struck me when a hail of cannon-shot from the guns which the Prussians had massed on a hill to the left, swept through us just as at Weissenfels; and that was not all. They had thirty pieces of artillery playing upon us. One can imagine from this what gaps they made. The balls shrieked sometimes over our heads, sometimes through the ranks, and then again struck the earth, which they scattered over us.

Our heavy guns replied to their fire with a vigor which kept us from hearing one half the hissing and roaring of theirs, but could not silence it, and the horrible cry of "Close up the ranks!" Close up the ranks!" was ever sounding in our ears.

We were enveloped in smoke without having fired a shot, and I said to myself, "if we stay here another quarter of an hour we shall all be massacred without having a chance to defend ourselves," which seemed to me fearful, when the head of the Prussian columns appeared between the hills, moving forward with a deep, hoarse murmur, like the noise of an inundation. Then the three first sides of our square, the second and the third obliquing to the right and left, fired. God only knows how many Prussians fell.

But instead of stopping they rushed on, shouting like wolves, "*Vaterland! Vaterland!*" and we fired again into their very bosoms.

Then began the work of death in earnest, Bayonet-thrust, sabre-stroke, blows from the butt-end of our pieces, crashed on all sides. They tried to crush us by mere weight of numbers, and came on like furious bulls. A battalion rushed upon us, thrusting with their bayonets; we returned their blows without leaving the ranks, and they were swept away almost to a man by two cannon which were in position fifty paces in our rear.

They were the last who tried to break our squares. They turned and fled down the hillside. and we were loading our guns to kill every man of them, when their pieces again opened fire, and we heard a great noise on our right. It was their cavalry charging. under cover of their fire. I could not see the fight, for it was at the other end of the division, but their heavy guns swept us off by dozens as we stood inactive. General Chemineau had his thigh broken; we could not hold out much longer when the order was given to retreat, which we did with a pleasure easily understood!

We retired to Gross-Gorschen, pursued by the

Prussians, both sides maintaining a constant fire. The two thousand men in the village checked the enemy while we ascended the opposite slope to gain Klein-Gorschen. But the Prussian cavalry came on once more to cut off our retreat and keep us under the fire of their artillery. Then my blood boiled with anger, and I heard Zébédé cry, "Let us fight our way to the top rather than remain here!"

To do this was fearfully dangerous, for their regiments of hussars and chasseurs advanced in good order to charge. Still we kept retreating, when a voice on the top of the ridge cried: "Halt!" and at the same moment the hussars, who were already rushing down upon us, received a terrific discharge of case and grape-shot, which swept them down by hundreds. It was Girard's division, who had come to our assistance from Klein-Gorschen and had placed sixteen pieces in position to open upon them. The hussars fled faster than they came, and the six squares of Girard's division united with ours at Klein-Gorschen, to check the Prussian infantry, which still continued to advance, the three first columns in front and three others, equally strong, supporting them.

We had lost Gross-Gorschen, but now, between Klein-Gorschen and Rahna the battle raged more fiercely than ever.

I thought now of nothing but vengeance. I was wild with excitement and wrath against those who sought to kill me. I felt a sort of hatred against those Prussians whose shouts and insolent manner disgusted me. I was, nevertheless, very glad to see Zébédé near me yet, and as we stood awaiting new attacks, with our arms resting on the ground, I pressed his hand.

"We have escaped narrowly enough," said he. "God grant the Emperor may soon arrive, and with cannon, for they are twenty times stronger than we."

He no longer spoke of winning the cross.

I looked around to see if the sergeant was with us yet, and saw him calmly wiping his bayonet; not a feature showed any trace of excitement—that encouraged me. I would have wished to know if Klipfel and Furst were unhurt, but the command, "Carry arms!" made me think of myself.

The three first columns of the enemy had halted on the hill of Gross-Gorschen to await their supports. The village in the valley between us was on fire, the flames bursting from the thatched roofs and the smoke rising to the sky, and to the left across the ploughed field we saw a long line of cannon coming down to open upon us.

It might have been mid-day when the six columns began their march and deployed masses of hussars and cavalry on both sides of Gross-Gorschen. Our artillery, placed behind the squares on the top of the ridge, opened a terrible fire on the Prussian gunners, who replied all along their line.

Our drums began to beat in the squares to give warning that the enemy were approaching, but their rattle was like the buzz of a fly in the storm, while in the valley the Prussians shouted altogether, "*Vaterland! Vaterland!*"

Their fire by battalion, as they climbed the hill, enveloped us in smoke—as the wind blew toward us—and hindered us from seeing them. Nevertheless, we began our file-firing. We heard and saw nothing but the noise and smoke of battle for the next quarter of an hour, when suddenly the Prussian hussars were in our square. I know not how it happened, but there they were on their little horses, sabring us without mercy.

We fought with our bayonets; we shouted; they slashed, and fired their pistols. The carnage was horrible. Zébédé, Sergeant Pinto, and some twenty of the company held together. I shall see all my life long the pale-faced, long-moustached hussars, the straps of their shakos tight under their jaws, whose horses reared and neighed as they dashed over the heaps of dead and wounded. I remember the cries, French and German in a horrid mixture, that arose; how they called us "*Schweinpelz*," and how old Pinto never ceased to cry, "Strike bravely, my boys; strike bravely!"

I never knew how we escaped; we ran at random through the smoke, and dashed through the midst of sabres and flying bullets. I only remember that Zébédé every moment cried out to me, "Come on! come on!" and that at last we found ourselves on a hillside behind a square which yet held firm, with Sergeant Pinto and seven or eight others of the company.

We were covered with blood, and looked like butchers.

"Load!" cried the sergeant.

Then I saw blood and hair on my bayonet, and I knew that in my fury I must have given some terrible blows. In a moment Old Pinto said, "The regiment is totally routed; the beggarly Prussians have sabred half of it; we shall find the remainder by and by. Now," he cried, "we must keep the enemy out of the village. By file, left! March!"

We descended a little stairway which led to one of the gardens of Klein-Gorschen, and entering a house, the sergeant barricaded the door leading to the fields with a heavy kitchen table; then he showed us the door opening on the street, telling us, "Here is our way of retreat." This done, we went to the floor above, and found a pretty large room, with two windows looking out upon the village, and two upon the hill, which was still covered with smoke and resounding with the crash of musketry and artillery. At one end in an alcove was a broken bedstead, and near it a cradle. The people of the house had no doubt fled at the beginning of the battle, but a dog, with ears erect and flashing eyes, glared at us from beneath the curtains. All this comes back to me like a dream.

The sergeant opened the window and fired at two or three Prussian hussars who were already advancing down the street. Zébédé and the others standing behind him stood ready. I looked toward the hill to see if the squares had yet remained unbroken, and I saw them retreating in good order, firing as they went from all four sides on the masses of cavalry which surrounded them completely. Through the smoke I could perceive the colonel on horseback, sabre in hand, and by him the colors, so torn by shot that they were mere rags hanging on the staff.

Beyond, on the left, a column of the enemy were debouching from the road and marching on Klein-Gorschen. This column evidently designed cutting off our retreat on the village, but hundreds of disbanded soldiers like us had arrived, and were pouring in from all sides; some turning ever and anon to fire, others wounded, trying to crawl to some place of shelter. They took possession of the houses, and, as the column approached, musketry rattled upon them from all the windows. This checked the enemy, and at the same moment the divisions of Brenier and Marchand, which the Prince of Moskowa had dispatched to our assistance, began to deploy to the right. We heard afterward that Marshal Ney had followed the Emperor in the direction of Leipzig and came back on hearing the sound of cannon.

The Prussians halted, and the firing ceased on both sides. Our squares and columns began to climb the hills again, opposite Starsiedel, and the defenders of the village rushed from the houses to join their regiments. Ours had become mingled with two or three others; and, when the reinforcing divisions halted before Kaya, we could scarcely find our places. The roll was called, and of our company but forty-two men remained; Furst and Leger were dead, but Zébédé, Klipfel, and I were unhurt.

But, unluckily, the battle was not yet over, for the Prussians, flushed with victory, were already making their dispositions to attack us at Kaya; reinforcements were hurrying to them, and it seemed that, for so great a general, the Emperor had made a gross blunder in stretching his lines to Leipzig, and leaving us to be overpowered by an army of over a hundred thousand men.

As we were re-forming behind Brenier's division, eighteen thousand veterans of the Prussian guard charged up the hill, carrying the shakos of our killed on their bayonets in token of victory. Once more the fight began, the mass of Russian cavalry, which we had seen glittering in the sun in the morning, came down on our flank,—on the left, between Klein-Gorschen and Starsiedel,—but the Sixth corps had arrived in time to cover it, and stood the shock like a castle wall. Once more shouts, groans, the clashing of sabre against bayonet, the crash of musketry and thunder of cannon shook the sky, while the plain was hidden in a cloud of smoke, through which we could see the glitter of helmets, cuirasses, and thousands of lances.

We were retiring, when something passed along our front like a flash of lightning. It was Marshal Ney surrounded by his staff. I never saw such a countenance; his eyes sparkled and his lips trembled with rage. In a second's time he had dashed along the lines, and drew up in front of our columns. The retreat stopped at once; he called us on, and, as if led by a kind of fascination, we dashed on to meet the Prussians, cheering like madmen as we went. But the Prussian line stood firm; they fought hard to keep the victory they had won, and besides were constantly receiving reinforcements, while we were worn out with five hours' fighting.

Our battalion was now in the second line, and the enemy's shot passed over our heads; but a horrible din made my flesh creep; it was the rattling of the grape-shot among the bayonets.

In the midst of shouts, orders, and the whistling of bullets, we again began to fall back over heaps of dead; our first division re-entered Klein-Gorschen, and once more the fight was hand to hand. In the main street of the village nothing was seen or heard but shots and blows, and generals, mounted, fought sword in hand like private soldiers.

This lasted some minutes; we in the ranks, said, "all is well, all is well, now we are advancing;" but again they were reinforced, and we were obliged to continue our retreat, and unhappily in such haste that many did not stop until they reached Kaya. This village was on the ridge and the last before reaching Lutzen. It is a long, narrow lane of houses, separated from each other by little gardens, stables and bee-hives. If the enemy forced us to Kaya, our army was cut in two. I recalled the words of M. Goulden—"If unluckily the allies get the best of us, they will revenge themselves on us in our own country for all we have been doing to them the last ten years." The battle seemed irretrievably lost, for Marshal Ney himself, in the centre of a square, was retreating; and many soldiers, to get away from the *melée*, were carrying off wounded officers on their muskets. Everything looked gloomy, indeed.

I entered Kaya on the right of the village, leaping over hedges, and creeping under the fences which separated the gardens, and was turning the corner of a street, when I saw some fifty officers on the brow of a hill before me, and behind them masses of artillery galloping at full speed along the Leipzig road. Then I saw the Emperor himself, a little in advance of the others; he was seated, as if in an arm-chair, on his white horse, and I could see him well, beneath the clear sky, motionless and looking at the battle through his field-glass.

My heart beat gladly; I cried "*Vive l'Empereur!*" with all my strength, and rushed along the main street of Kaya. I was one of the first to enter, and I saw the inhabitants of the village, men, women, and children, hastening to the cellars for protection.

Many to whom I have related the foregoing have sneered at me for running so fast; but I can only reply that when Michel Ney retreated, it was high time for Joseph Bertha to do so too.

Klipfel, Zébédé, Sergeant Pinto, and the others of the company had not yet arrived, when masses of black smoke arose above the roofs; shattered tiles fell into the streets, and shot buried themselves in the walls, or crashed through the beams with a horrible noise.

At the same time, our soldiers rushed in through the lanes, over the hedges and fences, turning from time to time to fire on the enemy. Men of all arms were mingled, some without shakos or knapsacks, their clothes torn and covered with blood; but they retreated furiously, and were nearly all mere children, boys of fifteen or twenty; but courage is inborn in the French people.

The Prussians—led by old officers who shouted '*Forwärts! Forwärts!*"—followed like packs of wolves, but we turned and opened fire from the hedges, and fences, and houses. How many of them bit the dust I know not, but others always supplied the places of those who fell. Hundreds of balls whistled by our ears and flattened themselves on the stone walls; the plaster was broken from the walls, and the thatch hung from the rafters, and as I turned for the twentieth time to fire, my musket dropped from my hand; I stooped to lift it, but I fell too: I had received a shot in the left shoulder and the blood ran like warm water down my breast. I tried to rise, but all that

I could do was to seat myself against the wall while the blood continued to run down even to my thighs, and I shuddered at the thought that I was to die there.

Still the fight went on.

Fearful that another bullet might reach me, I crawled to the corner of a house, and fell into a little trench which brought water from the street to the garden. My left arm was heavy as lead; my head swam; I still heard the firing, but it seemed a dream, and I closed my eyes.

When I again opened them, night was coming on, and the Prussians filled the village. In the garden, before me, was an old general, with white hair, on a tall brown horse. He shouted in a trumpet-like voice to bring on the cannon, and officers hurried away with his orders. Near him, standing on a little wall, two surgeons were bandaging his arm. Behind, on the other side, was a little Russian officer, whose plume of green feathers almost covered his hat. I saw all this at a glance—the old man with his large nose and broad forehead, his quick glancing eyes, and bold air; the others around him; the surgeon, a little bald man with spectacles, and five or six hundred paces away, between two houses, our soldiers re-forming.

The firing had ceased, but between Klein-Gorschen and Kaya terrible cries arose, and I could hear the heavy rumbling of artillery, neighing of horses, cries and shouts of drivers, and cracking of whips. Without knowing why, I dragged myself to the wall, and scarcely had I done so, when two sixteen pounders, each drawn by six horses, turned the corner of the street. The artillery-men beat the horses with all their strength, and the wheels rolled over the heaps of dead and wounded as if they were going over straw. Now I knew whence came the cries I had heard, and my hair stood on end with horror.

"Here!" cried the old man in German; "aim yonder, between those two houses near the fountain."

The two guns were turned at once; the old man, his left arm in a sling, cantered up the street, and I heard him say, in short, quick tones, to the young officer as he passed where I lay:

"Tell the Emperor Alexander that I am at Kaya. The battle is won if I am reinforced. Let them not discuss the matter, but send help at once. Napoleon is coming, and in half an hour we will have him upon us with his Guard.

I will stand, let it cost what it may. But in God's name do not lose a minute, and the victory is ours!"

The young man set off at a gallop, and at the same moment a voice near me whispered:

"That old wretch is Blücher. Ah, scoundrel! if I only had my gun!"

Turning my head, I saw an old sergeant, withered and thin, with long wrinkles in his cheeks, sitting against the door of the house, supporting himself with his hands on the ground, as with a pair of crutches, for a ball had passed through him from side to side. His yellow eyes followed the Prussian general; his hooked nose seemed to droop like the beak of an eagle over his thick moustache, and his look was fierce and proud.

"If I had my musket," he repeated, "I would show you whether the battle is won."

We were the only two living beings among heaps of dead.

I thought that perhaps I should be buried in the morning with the others, in the garden opposite us, and that I would never again see Catharine; the tears ran down my cheeks, and I could not help murmuring:

"Now all is indeed ended!"

The sergeant gazed at me and, seeing that I was yet so young, said kindly:

"What is the matter with you, conscript?"

"A ball in the shoulder, *mon sergeant.*"

"In the shoulder! That is better than one through the body. You will get over it."

And after a moment's thought he continued:

"Fear nothing. You will see home again!"

I thought that he pitied my youth and wished to console me; but my chest seemed crushed, and I could not hope.

The sergeant said no more, only from time to time he raised his head to see if our columns were coming. He swore between his teeth and ended by falling at length upon the ground, saying:

"My business is done! But the villain has paid for it!"

He gazed at the hedge opposite, where a Prussian grenadier was stretched, cold and stiff, the old sergeant's bayonet yet in his body.

It might then have been six in the evening. The enemy filled all the houses, gardens, orchards, the main streets and the alleys. I was cold and had dropped my head forward upon my knees, when the roll of artillery called me again to my senses. The two pieces in the garden and many others posted behind them threw their broad flashes through the darkness, while Russians and Prussians crowded through the street. But all this was as nothing in comparison to the fire of the French, from the hill opposite the village, while the constant glare showed the Young Guard coming on at the doublequick, generals and colonels on horseback in the midst of the bayonets, waving their swords and cheering them on, while the twenty-four guns the Emperor had sent to support the movement thundered behind. The old wall against which I leaned shook to its foundations. In the street the balls mowed down the enemy like grass before the scythe. It was their turn to close up the ranks.

I also heard the enemy's artillery replying behind us, and I thought, "Heaven grant that the French win the day; then their suffering wounded will be taken care of, instead of these Prussians and Cossacks first looking after their own, and leaving us all to perish."

I paid no further attention to the sergeant, I only looked at the Prussian gunners loading their guns, aiming and firing them, cursing them all the time from the bottom of my heart, but all the time listening to the inspiring shouts of "*Vive l'Empereur!*" ringing out in the momentary silence between the reports of the guns.

In about twenty minutes the Russians and Prussians were forced to fall back; going in crowds by the narrow passage where we were; the shouts of "*Vive l'Empereur!*" grew nearer and nearer. The cannoneers at the pieces before me loaded and fired at their utmost speed, when three or four grape-shots fell among them and broke the wheel of one of their guns, besides killing two and wounding another of their men. I felt a hand seize my arm. It was the old sergeant. His eyes were glazing in death, but he laughed scornfully and savagely. The roof of our shelter fell in; the walls bent, but we cared not, we only saw the defeat of the enemy and heard the shouts of our men nearer and nearer, when the old sergeant gasped in my ear:

"Here he is!"

He rose to his knees, supporting himself with one hand, while with the other he waved his hat in the air, and cried in a ringing voice:

" *Vive l'Empereur!*"

Then he fell on his face to the earth, and moved no more.

And I, raising myself too from the ground, saw Napoleon, riding calmly through the hail of shot—his hat pulled down over his large head—his gray great-coat open, a broad red ribbon crossing his white vest—there he rode, calm and imperturbable, his face lit up with the reflection from the bayonets. None stood their ground before *him;* the Prussian artillerymen abandoned their pieces and sprang over the garden-hedge, despite the cries of their officers who sought to keep them back.

All this I saw—it seems graved with fire on my memory, but from that moment I can remember no more of the battle, for in that certainty of victory I lost consciousness and fell like a corpse in the midst of corpses.

XIV.

WHEN sense returned it was night and all was silent around. Clouds were scudding across the sky, and the moon shone down upon the abandoned village, the broken guns, and the pale upturned faces of the dead, as calmly as for ages she had looked on the flowing water, the waving grass, and the rustling leaves which fall in autumn. Men are but insects in the midst of creation; lives but drops in the ocean of eternity, and none so truly feel their insignificance as the dying.

I could not move from where I lay in the intensest pain. My right arm alone could I stir; and raising myself with difficulty upon my elbow, I saw the dead heaped along the street, their white faces shining like snow in the moonlight. The mouths and eyes of some were wide open others lay on their faces, their knapsacks and cartridge-boxes on their backs and their hands grasping their muskets. The sight thrilled me with horror, and my teeth chattered.

I would have cried for help but my voice was no louder than that of a sobbing child. But my feeble cry awoke others, and groans and shrieks arose on all sides. The wounded thought succor was coming, and all who could cried piteously. These cries lasted some time; then all was silent, and I only heard a horse neigh painfully on the other side of the hedge. The poor animal tried to rise, and I saw its head and long neck appear; then it fell again to the earth.

The effort I made reopened my wound, and again I felt the blood running down my arm. I closed my eyes to die, and the scenes of my early childhood, of my native village, the face of my poor mother as she sang me to sleep, my little room, with its alcove, our old dog Pommer with whom I used to play and roll over and over on the ground; my father as he came home gaily in the evening, his axe on his shoulder, and took me up in his strong arms to embrace me—all rose dreamily before me.

How little those parents thought that they

were rearing their boy to die miserably far from friends, and home, and succor! How great would have been their desolation—what maledictions would they have poured on those who reduced him to such a state! Ah! if they were but there!—if I could have asked their forgiveness for all the pain I had given them! As these thoughts rushed over me the tears rolled down my cheeks; my heart heaved: I sobbed like a child.

Then Catharine, Aunt Grédel, and Monsieur Goulden passed before me. I saw their grief and fear when the news of the battle came. Aunt Grédel running to the post-office every day to learn something of me, and Catherine prayerfully awaiting her return, while Monsieur Goulden read in the gazette how the Third corps suffered more heavily than the others, as he paced the room with drooping head and at last sat dreamily at his work-bench. My heart was with them; it followed Aunt Grédel to the post-office, and returned with her all sadly to the village, and there it saw Catharine in her despairing grief.

Then the postman Roedig seemed to arrive at Quatre-Vents. He opened his leathern sack, and handed a large paper to Aunt Grédel, while Catharine stood pale as death beside her. It was the official notice of my death : I heard Catharine's heart-rending cries as she fell swooning to the ground, and Aunt Grédel's maledictions, as, with her gray hair streaming about her head, she cried that justice was no longer to be found —that it were better that we had never been born, since even God seemed to have abandoned us. Good Father Goulden came to console them, but could only sob too : all wept together in their desolation, crying :

"Joseph! Poor, poor Joseph!"

My heart seemed bursting.

The thought came that thirty or forty thousand families in France, in Russia, in Germany, were soon to receive the same news—news yet more terrible, for many of the wretches stretched on the battle-field had father and mother, and this was horrible to think of—it seemed as if a wail from all human kind were rising from earth to Heaven.

Then I remembered those poor women of Phalsbourg, praying in the church when we heard of the retreat from Russia, and I understood how their hearts were torn. I thought that Catharine would soon go there, and year after year she would pray—thinking of me. Yes—for I knew we had loved each other from childhood, and that she could never forget me, and tear after tear coursed down my cheeks. This confidence soothed me in my grief—the certainty that she would preserve her love for me until age whitened her hair; that I should be ever before her eyes, and that she would never marry another.

Toward morning a shower began to fall, and the monotonous dropping on the roofs alone broke the silence. I thought of the good God, whose power and mercy are limitless, and I hoped that He would pardon my sins in consideration of my sufferings.

The rain filled the little trench in which I had been lying. From time to time a wall fell in the village, and the cattle, scared away by the battle, began to resume confidence and return. I heard a goat bleat in a neighboring stable. A great shepherd's dog wandered fearfully among the heaps of dead. The horse, seeing him, neighed in terror—he took him for a wolf—and the dog fled.

I remember all these details, for, when we are dying, we see everything, we hear everything, for we know that we are seeing and hearing our last.

But how my whole frame thrilled with joy when, at the corner of the street, I thought I heard the sound of voices! How eagerly I listened! And I raised myself upon my elbow, and called for help. It was yet night; but the first grey streak of day was becoming visible in the east, and afar off, through the falling rain, I saw a light in the fields, now coming onward, now stopping. I saw dark forms bending around it. They were only confused shadows. But others beside me saw the light; for on all sides arose groans and plaintive cries, from voices so feeble that they seemed like those of children calling their mothers.

What is this life to which we attach so great a price? This miserable existence, so full of pain and suffering? Why do we so cling to it, and fear more to lose it than aught else in the world? What is it that is to come hereafter that makes us shudder at the mere thought of death? Who knows? For ages and ages all have thought and thought on the great question, but none have yet solved it. I, in my eagerness to live, gazed on that light as the drowning man looks to the shore. I could not take my eyes from it, and my heart thrilled with hope. I tried again to shout, but my voice died on my lips. The pattering of the rain on the ruined dwellings, and on the trees, and on the ground, drowned all other sounds, and, although I kept repeating "They hear us! They are coming!" and although the lantern seemed to grow larger and larger, after wandering for some time over the field, it slowly disappeared behind a little hill.

I fell once more senseless to the ground.

XV.

When I returned to myself, I looked around. I was in a long hall, with posts all around. Some one gave me wine and water to drink, and it was most grateful. I was in a bed, and beside me was an old gray-moustached soldier, who, when he saw my eyes open, lifted up my head and held a cup to my lips.

"Well," said he cheerfully, "well! we are better."

I could not help smiling as I thought that I was yet among the living. My chest and arm were stiff with bandages; I felt as if a hot iron were burning me there; but no matter, I lived!

I gazed at the heavy rafters crossing the space above me; at the tiles of the roof, through which the daylight entered in more than one spot; I turned and looked to the other side, and saw that I was in of one those vast sheds used by the brewers of the country as a shelter for their casks and wagons. All around, on mattresses and heaps of straw, numbers of wounded lay ranged; and in the middle, on a large kitchen-table, a surgeon-major and his two aids, their shirt-sleeves rolled up, were amputating the leg of a soldier, who was shrieking in agony. Behind them was a mass of legs and arms. I turned away sick and trembling.

Five or six soldiers were walking about, giving bread and drink to the wounded.

But the man who impressed himself most on my memory was a surgeon with sleeves rolled up, who cut and cut without paying the slightest attention to what was going on around; he was a man with a large nose and wrinkled cheeks, and every moment flew into a passion at his assistants, who could not give him his knives, pincers, lint, or linen fast enough, or who were not quick enough sponging up the blood.

Things went on quickly, however, for in less than a quarter of an hour he had cut off two legs.

Without, against the posts, was a large wagon full of straw.

They had just laid out on the table a Russian

carbineer, six feet in height at least; a ball had pierced his neck near the ear, and while the surgeon was asking for his little·knives, a cavalry surgeon passed before the shed. He was short, stout, and badly pitted with the small-pox, and held a portfolio under his arm.

"Ha! Forel!" cried he cheerfully.

"It is Duchêne," said our surgeon, turning around. "How many wounded?"

"Seventeen to eighteen thousand."

"Aha! Well, how goes it this morning?"

"Passably—I am looking for a tavern."

Our surgeon left the shed to chat with his comrade; they conversed quietly, while the assistants sat down to drink a cup of wine, and the Russian rolled his eyes despairingly.

"See, Duchêne; you have only to go down the street, opposite that well, do you see?"

"Very well indeed."

"Just opposite you will see the canteen."

"Very good; thank you; I am off."

He started, and our surgeon called after him:

"A good appetite to you Duchêne!"

Then he returned to his Russian, whose neck he laid open. He worked ill-humoredly, constantly scolding his aids.

"Be quick!" he said, "be quick!"

The Russian writhed and groaned, but he paid no attention to that, and at last, throwing the bullet upon the ground, he bandaged up the wound, and cried, "Carry him off!"

They lifted the Russian from the table, and stretched him on a mattress beside the others; then they laid his neighbor upon the table.

I could not think that such horrors took place in the world; but I was yet to see worse than this.

At five or six beds from mine sat an old corporal with his leg bound up. He closed one eye knowingly, and said to his neighbor, whose arm had just been cut off:

"Conscript, look at that heap! I will bet that you cannot recognize your arm."

The other, who had hitherto shown the greatest courage, looked, and fell back senseless.

Then the corporal began laughing, saying:

He has recognized it. It is the lower one, with the little blue flower. It always produces that effect."

He looked around self-approvingly, but no one laughed with him.

Every moment the wounded called for water.

"Drink! Drink!"

When one began, all followed, and the old soldier had certainly conceived a liking for me, for each time he passed, he presented the cup.

I did not remain in the shed more than an hour. A dozen ambulances drew up before the door, and the peasants of the country round, in their velvet jackets, and large black slouched hats, their whips on their shoulders, held the horses by the reins. A picket of hussars arrived soon after, and their officer dismounting, entered and said:

"Excuse me, major, but here is an order to escort twelve wagons of wounded as far as Lutzen. Is it here that we are to receive them?"

"Yes, it is here," replied the surgeon.

The peasants and the ambulance-drivers, after giving us a last draught of wine, began carrying us to the wagons. As one was filled, it departed, and another advanced. I was in the third, seated on the straw, in the front row, beside a conscript of the Twenty-seventh, who had lost his right hand; behind was another who had lost a leg; then came one whose head was laid open, and another whose jaw was broken; so was the wagon filled.

They had given us our great coats; but despite

them and the sun, which was shining brightly, we shivered with cold, and left only our noses and forage-caps, or linen bandages on the splints visible. No one spoke; each was too much occupied thinking of himself.

At moments I was terribly cold; then flashes of heat would dart through me, and flush me as in a fever; and indeed it was the beginning of the fever. But as we left Kaya, I was yet well; I saw everything clearly, and it was not until we neared Leipzig that I felt indeed sick.

At last we were all placed in the wagons, and arranged according to our condition—those able to sit up, in the first that set out, the others stretched in the last, and we started. The hussars rode beside us, smoking and chatting, paying no attention to us.

In passing through Kaya, I saw all the horrors of war. The village was but a mass of cinders; the roofs had fallen, and the walls alone remained standing; the rafters were broken; we could see the remnants of rooms, stairs, and doors heaped within. The poor villagers, women, children, and old men, came and went with sorrowful faces. We could see them going up and down in their houses, as if they were in cages in the open air; and in one we saw a mirror and an evergreen branch, showing where dwelt a young girl in time of peace.

Ah! who could foresee that their happiness would so soon be destroyed, not by the fury of the winds or the wrath of heaven, but by the rage of man!

Even the cattle and pigeons seemed seeking their lost homes among the ruins; the oxen and the goats, scattered through the streets, lowed and bleated plaintively. Fowls were roosting upon the trees, and everywhere, everywhere we saw the traces of cannon-balls.

At the last house an old man with flowing white hair, sat at the threshold of what had been his cottage, with a child upon his knees, glaring on us as we passed. "Did he see us?" I do not know. His furrowed brow and stony eyes spoke of despair. How many years of labor, of patient economy, of suffering, had he passed to make sure a quiet old age! Now all was crushed, ruined; the child and he had no longer a roof to cover their heads.

And those great trenches—fully a mile of them —at which the country people were working in such haste, to keep the plague from completing the work war began! I saw them, too, from the top of the hill of Kaya, and turned away my eyes, horror-stricken. Russians, French, Prussians were there heaped pell-mell, as if God had made them to love each other before the invention of arms and uniforms, which divide them for the profit of those who rule them. There they lay, side by side; and the part of them which could not die knew no more of war, but cursed the crimes that had for centuries kept them apart.

But what was sadder yet, was the long line of ambulances, bearing the agonized wounded—those of whom they speak so much in the bulletins to make the loss seem less, and who die by thousands in the hospitals, far from all they love; while at their homes cannon are firing, and church-bells are ringing with joyous chimes—rejoicing that thousands of men are slain!

At length we reached Lutzen, but it was so full of wounded that we were obliged to continue on to Leipzig. We saw in the streets only half-dead wretches, stretched on straw along the walls of the houses. It was more than an hour before we reached a church, where fifteen or twenty of us who could no longer proceed were left.

Our ambulance conductor and his men, after refreshing themselves at a tavern at the street corner, remounted, and we continued our journey to Leipzig.

I saw and heard no more; my head swam; a murmuring filled my ears, I thought trees were men, and an intolerable thirst burned my lips.

For a long while past, many in the wagons had been shrieking, calling upon their mothers, trying to rise and fling themselves upon the road. I know not whether I did the same; but I awoke as from a horrible dream, as two men seized me, each by a leg, placing their arms under my body, and carried me through a dark square. The sky seemed covered with stars, and innumerable lights shone from an immense edifice before us. It was the hospital of the market-place at Leipzig.

The two men who were carrying me ascended a spiral stairway which led to an immense hall where beds were laid together in three lines, so close that they touched each other. On one of these beds I was placed, in the midst of oaths, cries for pity, and muttered complaints from hundreds of fever-stricken wounded. The windows were open, and the flames of the lanterns flickered in the gusts of wind. Surgeons, assistants, and nurses with great aprons tied beneath their arms, came and went, while the groans from the halls below, and the rolling of ambulances, cracking of whips and neighing of horses without, seemed to pierce my very brain. While they were undressing me, they handled me roughly, and my wound pained me so horribly that I could not avoid shrieking. A surgeon came up at once, and scolded them for not being more careful. That is all I remember that night; for I became delirious, and raved constantly of Catharine, Monsieur Goulden, and Aunt Grédel, as my neighbor, an old artilleryman, whom my cries prevented from sleeping, afterward told me. I awoke the next morning at about eight o'clock, at the first roll of the drum, and saw the hall better, and then learned that I had the bone of my left shoulder broken. A dozen surgeons were around me; one of them, a stout, dark man, whom they called Monsieur the Baron, was opening my bandages, while an assistant at the foot of the bed held a basin of warm water. The baron examined my wound; all the others bent forward to hear what he might say. He spoke a few moments, but all that I could understand was, that the ball had struck from below, breaking the bone and passing out behind. I saw that he knew his business well, for the Prussians had fired from below, over the garden wall, so that the ball must have ranged upward. He washed the wound himself, and with a couple of turns of his hand, replaced the bandage, so that my shoulder could not move, and everything was in order.

I felt much better. Ten minutes after a hospital steward put a shirt on me without hurting me—such was his skill.

The surgeon, passing to another bed, cried:

"What! You here again, old fellow?"

"Yes; it is I, Monsieur the Baron," replied the artilleryman, proud to be recognized; "the first time was at Austerlitz, the second at Jena, and then I received two thrusts of a lance at Smolensk."

"Yes, yes," said the surgeon kindly; "and now what is the matter with you?"

"Three sabre-cuts on my left arm while I was defending my piece from the Prussian hussars."

The surgeon unwound the bandage, and asked:

"Have you the cross?"

"No, Monsieur the Baron."

"What is your name?"

"Christian Zimmer, of the Second horse artillery."

"Very good!"

He dressed the wounds, and went to the next, saying:

"You will soon be well."

He returned, chatting with the others, and went out after finishing his round and giving some orders to the nurses.

The old artilleryman's heart seemed overflowing with joy; and, as I concluded from his name that he came from Alsace, I spoke to him in our language, at which he was still more rejoiced. He was a tall fellow—at least six feet in height, with round shoulders, a flat forehead, large nose, light red moustaches, and was as hard as a rock, but a good man for all that. His eyes twinkled when I spoke Alsatian to him, and he pricked up his ears at once. If I asked him in our tongue he was willing to give me everything he had, but he had only a clasp of the hand which cracked the bones in mine to give. He called me *Josephel*, as they did at home, and said:

"Josephel, be careful how you swallow the medicines they give you, only take what you know. All that does not smell good is good for nothing. If they would give us a bottle of *Rikevir* every day we would soon be well; but it is easier to spoil our digestion with a handful of vile boiled herbs, than to bring us a little of the good white wine of Alsace."

When I told him I was afraid of dying of the fever, he looked angry with his great gray eyes, and said:

"Josephel, you are a fool. Do you think that such tall fellows as you and I were born to die in a hospital? No, no; drive the idea from your head."

But he spoke in vain, for every morning the surgeons, making their rounds, found seven or eight dead. Some died in fevers, some in deadly chill; so that heat or cold might be the presage of death.

Zimmer said that all this proceeded from the evil drugs which the doctors invented. "Do you see that tall, thin fellow?" he asked. "Well, that man can boast of having killed more men than a field-piece; he is always primed, with his match lighted; and that little brown fellow—I would send him instead of the Emperor to the

Russians and Prussians; he would kill more of them than a whole army corps."

He would have made me laugh with his jokes if the litters had not been constantly passing.

At the end of three weeks my shoulder began to heal, and Zimmer's wounds were also doing well. They gave us every morning some good boiled beef which warmed our hearts, and in the evening a little beef with half a glass of wine, the sight alone of which rejoiced us and made the future look hopeful.

About this time, too, they allowed us to walk in the large garden, full of elms, behind the hospital. There were benches under the trees, and we walked the paths like millionaires in our gray great-coats and forage-caps. The weather was magnificent; and we could see far along the poplar bordered Partha. This river falls into the Elster, on the left, forming a long blue line. On the same side stretches a forest of beech trees, and in front are three or four great white roads, which cross fields of wheat, barley and hay, and hop plantations; no sight could be pleasanter, or richer, especially when the breeze falls upon it and these harvests rise and fall in the sunlight like waves of the sea. The

"WHAT MAKES YOU CRY SO, JOSEPHEL?" (Page 219.)

increasing heat presaged a fine year, and often, when looking at the beautiful scenery around, I thought of Phalsbourg; and the tears came to my eyes.

"I would like to know what makes you cry so, Josephel," said Zimmer. "Instead of catching a fever in the hospital, or losing a leg or arm, like hundreds of others, here we are quietly seated in the shade; we are well fed, and can smoke when we have any tobacco; and still you cry. What more do you want, Josephel?"

Then I told him of Catharine; of our walks at Quatre-Vents; of our promises; of all my former life, which then seemed a dream. He listened, smoking his pipe.

"Yes, yes," said he; "all this is very sad. Before the conscription of 1798, I too was going to marry a girl of our village, who was named Margrédel, and whom I loved better than all the world beside. We had promised to marry each other, and all through the campaign of Zurich, I never passed a day without thinking of her. But when I first received a furlough and reached home, what did I hear? Margrédel had been three months married to a shoemaker, named Passauf."

You may imagine my wrath, Josephel; I could not see clearly; I wanted to demolish everything; and, as they told me that Passauf was at the *Grand-Cerf* brewery, thither I started, looking neither to the right nor left. There I saw him drinking with three or four rogues. As I rushed forward, he cried, 'There comes Christian Zimmer! How goes it, Christian? Margrédel sends you her compliments.' He winked his eye. I seized a glass, which I hurled at his head, and broke to pieces, saying, 'Give her that for my wedding present, you beggar!' The others, seeing their friend thus maltreated, very naturally fell upon me. I knocked two or three of them over with a jug, jumped on a table, sprang through a window, and beat a retreat."

"It was time," I thought.

"But that was not all," he continued; "I had scarcely reached my mother's when the gendarmerie arrived, and they arrested me. They put me on a wagon and conducted me from brigade to brigade until we reached my regiment, which was at Strasbourg. I remained six weeks at Finckmatt, and would probably have received the ball and chain, if we had not had to cross the Rhine to Hohenlinden.

"The Commandant Courtaud himself said to me:

"'You can boast of striking a hard blow, but if you happen again to knock people over with jugs, it will not be well for you—I warn you. Is that any way to fight, animal? Why do we wear sabres, if not to use them and do our country honor?'

"I had no reply to make.

"From that day, Josephel, the thought of marriage never troubled me. Don't talk to me of a soldier who has a wife to think of. Look at our generals who are married, do they fight as they used to? No, they have but one idea, and that is to increase their store and to profit by their wealth by living well with their duchesses and little dukes at home. My grandfather Yéri, the forester, always said that a good hound should be lean, and I think the same of good generals and good soldiers. The poor fellows are always in working order, but our generals grow fat from their good dinners at home."

So spoke my friend Zimmer in the honesty of his heart, and all this did not lessen my sadness.

As soon as I could sit up, I hastened to in-form Monsieur Goulden, by letter, that I was in the hospital of Halle, in one of the five buildings of Leipzig, slightly wounded in the arm, but that he need fear nothing for me, for I was growing better and better. I asked him to show my letter to Catharine and Aunt Grédel to comfort them in the midst of such fearful war. I told him, too, that my greatest happiness would be to receive news from home and of the health of all whom I loved.

From that moment I had no rest; every morning I expected an answer, and to see the postmaster distribute twenty or thirty letters in our ward, without my receiving one, almost broke my heart; I hurried to the garden and wept. There was a little dark corner where they threw broken pottery—a place buried in shade, which pleased me much, because no one ever came there—there I passed my time dreaming on an old moss-covered bench. Evil thoughts crossed my brain—I almost believed that Catherine could forget her promises, and I muttered to myself, "Ah! if you had not been picked up at Kaya! All would then have been ended! Why were you not abandoned? Better to have been, than to suffer thus!"

To such a pass did I finally arrive, that I no longer wished to recover, when one morning the letter-carrier, among other names, called that of Joseph Bertha. I lifted my hand without being able to speak, and a large, square letter, covered with innumerable post-marks, was handed me. I recognized Monsieur Goulden's hand-writing, and turned pale.

"Well," said Zimmer, laughing, "it is come at last."

I did not answer, but thrust the letter in my pocket, to read it at leisure and alone. I went to the end of the garden and opened it. Two or three apple-blossoms dropped upon the ground, with an order for money, on which Monsieur Goulden had written a few words. But what touched me most was the handwriting of Catharine, which I gazed at without reading a word, while my heart beat as if about to burst through my bosom.

At last I grew a little calmer and read the letter slowly, stopping from time to time to make sure that I made no mistake—that it was indeed my dear Catharine who wrote, and that I was not in a dream.

I have kept that letter, because it brought, so to

speak, life back to me. Here it is as I received it on the eighth day of June, 1813:

"My Dear Joseph:—I write you to tell you I yet love you alone, and that, day by day, I love you more.

"My greatest grief is to know that you are wounded, in a hospital, and that I cannot take care of you. Since the conscripts departed, we have not had a moment's peace of mind. My mother says I am silly to weep night and day, but she weeps as much as I, and her wrath falls heavily on Pinacle, who dared not come to the market-place, because she carried a hammer in her basket.

But our greatest grief was when we heard that the battle had taken place, and that thousands of men had fallen; mother ran every morning to the post-office, while I could not move from the house. At last your letter came, thank heaven! to cheer us. Now I am better, for I can weep at my ease, thanking God that He has saved your life.

"And when I think how happy we used to be, Joseph —when you came every Sunday, and we sat side by side without stirring and thought of nothing! Ah! we did not know how happy we were; we knew not what might happen—but God's will be done. If you only recover! if we may only hope to be once again as happy as we were!

"Many people talk of peace, but the Emperor so loves war, that I fear it is far off.

"What pleases me most is to know that your wound is

not dangerous, and that you still love me. Ah! Joseph, I will love you forever—that is all I can say. I can say it from the bottom of my heart; and I know my mother loves you too!

"Now, Monsieur Goulden wishes to say a few words to you, so I will close. The weather is beautiful here, and the great apple-tree in the garden is full of flowers; I have plucked a few, which I shall put in this letter when M. Goulden has written. Perhaps with God's blessing we shall yet eat together one of those large apples. Embrace me as I embrace you, Joseph, Farewell! Farewell!"

As I finished reading this, Zimmer arrived, and in my joy, I said:

"Sit down, Zimmer, and I will read you my sweetheart's letter. You will see whether she is a Margrédel."

"Let me light my pipe first," he answered; and having done so, he added: "Go on, Josephel, but I warn you that I am an old bird, and do not believe all I hear; women are more cunning than we."

Notwithstanding this bit of philosophy, I read Catharine's letter slowly to him. When I had ended, he took it, and for a long time gazed at it dreamily, and then handed it back, saying:

"There! Josephel. She *is* a good girl, and a

sensible one, and will never marry any one but you."

"Do you really think so?"

"Yes; you may rely upon her; she will never marry a Passauf. I would rather distrust the Emperor than such a girl."

I could have embraced Zimmer for these words; but I said:

"I have received a bill for one hundred francs. Now for some white wine of Alsace. Let us try to get out."

"That is well thought of," said he, twisting his moustache and putting his pipe in his pocket. "I do not like to mope in a garden when there are taverns outside. We must get permission."

We arose joyfully and went to the hospital, when the letter-carrier, coming out, stopped Zimmer, saying:

"Are you Christian Zimmer, of the Second horse artillery?"

"I have that honor, monsieur the carrier."

"Well, here is something for you," said the other, handing him a little package and a large letter.

Zimmer was stupefied, never having received anything from home or from anywhere else. He opened the packet—a box appeared—then the box —and saw the cross of honor. He became pale: his eyes filled with tears, he staggered against a balustrade, and then shouted "*Vive l'Empereur!*" in such tones that the three halls rang and rang again.

The carrier looked on smiling.

"You are satisfied," said he.

"Satisfied! I need but one thing more."

"And what is that?"

"Permission to go to the city."

"You must ask Monsieur Tardieu, the surgeon in chief."

He went away laughing, while we ascended arm-in-arm, to ask permission of the surgeon-major, an old man, who had heard the "*Vive l'Empereur!*" and demanded gravely:

"What is the matter?"

Zimmer showed his cross and replied:

"Pardon, major; but I am more than usually merry."

"I can easily believe you," said Monsieur Tardieu; "you want a pass to the city?"

"If you will be so good; for myself and my comrade, Joseph Bertha."

The surgeon had examined my wound the day

before. He took out his portfolio and gave us passes. We left as proud as kings—Zimmer of his cross, I, of my letter.

Down-stairs in the great vestibule the porter cried:

"Hold on there! Where are you going?"

Zimmer showed him our passes, and we sallied forth, glad to breathe the free air, without, once more. A sentinel showed us the post-office where I was to receive my hundred francs.

Then, more gravely, for our joy had sunk deeper in our hearts, we reached the gate of Halle about two muskets shots to the left, at the end of a long avenue of lindens. Each faubourg is separated from the old ramparts only by these avenues, and all around Leipzig passes another very wide one, also bordered with lindens. The ramparts are very old—such as we see at Saint Hippolyte, on the upper Rhine,—crumbling, grass-grown walls; at least such they are if the Germans have not repaired them since 1813.

XVI.

How much were we to learn that day! At the hospital no one troubled himself about anything: when every morning you see fifty wounded come in, and when every evening you see as many depart upon the bier, you have the world before you in a narrow compass, and you think—

"After us comes the end of the universe!"

But without, these ideas change. When I caught the first glimpse of the street of Halle,—that old city with its shops, its gateways filled with merchandise, its old peaked roofs, its heavy wagons laden with bales, in a word, all its busy commercial life,—I was struck with wonder; I had never seen anything like it, and I said to myself:

"This is indeed a mercantile city, such as they talk of—full of industrious people trying to make a living, or competence, or wealth; where every one seeks to rise, not to the injury of others, but by working—contriving night and day how to make his family prosperous; so that all profit by inventions and discoveries. Here is the happiness of peace in the midst of a fearful war!"

But the poor wounded, wandering about with their arms in slings, or perhaps dragging a leg after them as they limped on crutches, were sad sights to see.

I walked dreamily through the streets, led by Zimmer, who recognized every corner, and kept repeating:

"There—there is the church of Saint Nicholas; that large building is the university: that on yonder is the *Hôtel de Ville.*"

He seemed to remember every stone, having been there in 1807, before the battle of Friedland, and continued:

"We are the same here as if we were in Metz, or Strasbourg, or any other city in France. The people wish us well. After the campaign of 1806, they used to do all they could for us. The citizens would take three or four of us at a time to dinner with them. They even gave us balls and called us the heroes of Jena. Go where we would they everywhere received us as benefactors of the country. We named their elector King of Saxony, and gave him a good slice of Poland."

Suddenly he stopped before a little, low door, and cried:

"Hold! Here is the Golden Sheep Brewery. The front is on the other street, but we can enter here. Come!"

I followed him into a narrow, winding passage which led to an old court, surrounded by rubble walls, with little moss-covered galleries under the roof and a weathercock upon the peak, as in the Tanner's Lane in Strasbourg. To the right was the brewery, and in a corner a great wheel, turned by an enormous dog, which pumped the beer to every story of the house.

The clinking of glasses was heard coming from a room which opened on the Rue de Tilly, and under the windows of this was a deep cellar resounding with the cooper's hammer. The sweet smell of the new March beer filled the air, and Zimmer, with a look of satisfaction, cried:

"Yes, here I came six years ago with Ferré and stout Rousillon. How glad I am to see it all again, Josephel! It was six years ago. Poor Rousillon! he left his bones at Smolensk last year! and Ferré must now be at home in his village near Toul, for he lost his left leg at Wagram. How everything comes back as I think of it!"

At the same time he pushed open the door, and we entered a lofty hall, full of smoke. I saw, through the thick, gray atmosphere, a long row of tables, surrounded by men drinking—the greater number in short coats and little caps, the remainder in the Saxon uniform. The first were students, young men of family who came to Leipzig to study law, medicine, and all that can be learned by emptying glasses and leading a jolly life, which they call *Fuchs-commerce*. They often fight among themselves with a sort of blade rounded at the point and only its tip sharpened, so that they slash their faces, as Zimmer told me, but life is never endangered. This shows the good sense of these students, who know very well that life is precious, and that one had better get five or six slashes, or even more, than lose it.

Zimmer laughed as he told me these things; his love of glory blinded him; he said they might as well load cannon with roasted apples, as fight with swords rounded at the point.

But we entered the hall, and we saw the oldest of the students—a tall withered-looking man with a red nose and long flaxen beard, stained with beer—standing upon a table, reading the gazette aloud which hung from his hand like an apron. He held the paper in one hand, and in the other a long porcelain pipe. His comrades, with their long, light hair falling upon their shoulders, were listening with the deepest interest; and as we entered, they shouted "*Vaterland! Vaterland!*"

They touched glasses with the Saxon soldiers, while the tall student bent over to take up his glass, and the round, fat brewer cried:

"*Gesundheit! Gesundheit!*"

Scarcely had we made half a dozen steps toward them, when they became silent.

"Come, come, comrades!" cried Zimmer, don't disturb yourselves. Go on reading. We do not object to hear the news."

But they did not seem inclined to profit by our invitation, and the reader descended from the table, folding up his paper, which he put in his pocket.

"We are done," said he, "we are done."

"Yes; we are done," repeated the others, looking at each other with a peculiar expression.

Two or three of the German soldiers rose and left the room, as if to take the air in the court, and the fat landlord said:

"You do not perhaps know that the large hall is on the Rue de Tilly?"

"Yes; we know it very well," replied Zimmer; "but I like this little hall better. Here I used to come, long ago, with two old comrades, to empty a few glasses in honor of Jena and Auerstadt. I know this room of old."

"Ah! as you please, as you please," returned the landlord. "Do you wish some March beer?"

"Yes; two glasses and the gazette."

"Very good."

The glasses were handed us, and Zimmer, who observed nothing, tried to open a conversation with the students; but they excused themselves, and, one after another, went out. I saw that they hated us, but dared not show it.

The gazette, which was from France, spoke of an armistice, after two new victories at Bautzen and Wurtschen. This armistice commenced on the sixth of June, and a conference was then being held at Prague, in Bohemia, to arrange on terms of peace. All this naturally gave me pleasure. I thought of again seeing home. But

Zimmer, with his habit of thinking aloud, filled the hall with his reflections, and interrupted me at every line.

"An armistice!" he cried. "Do *we* want an armistice. After having beaten those Prussians and Russians at Lutzen, Bautzen and Wurtschen, ought we not to annihilate then? Would they give us an armistice if they had beaten us? There, Joseph, you see the Emperor's character —he is too good. It is his only fault. He did the same thing after Austerlitz, and he had to begin over again. I tell you, he is too good; and if he were not so, we should have been masters of Europe."

As he spoke, he looked around as if seeking assent; but the students scowled, and no one replied.

At last Zimmer rose.

"Come, Joseph," said he; "I know nothing of politics, but I insist that we should give no armistice to those beggars. When they are down, we should keep them there."

After we had paid our reckoning, and were once more in the street, he continued:

"I do not know what was the matter with those people to-day. We must have disturbed them in something."

"It is very possible," I replied. "They certainly did not seem like the good-natured folks you were speaking of."

"No," said he. "Those young fellows are far beneath the old students I have seen. *They* passed—I might say—their lives at the brewery. They drank twenty and sometimes thirty glasses a day; even I, Joseph, had no chance with such fellows. Five or six of them whom they called "seniors" had grey beards and a venerable appearance. We sang *Fanfan la Tulipe* and 'King Dagobert' together, which are not political songs, you know. But these fellows are good for nothing."

I knew afterward, that those students were members of the *Tugend-bund.*

On returning to the hospital, after having had a good dinner and drank a bottle of wine apiece in the inn of La Grappe in the Rue de Tilly, we learned that we were to go, that same evening, to the barracks of Rosenthal—a sort of depot for wounded, near Lutzen, where the roll was called morning and evening, but where, at all other times, we were at liberty to do as we pleased. Every three days, the surgeon made his visit; as soon as one was well, he received his order to march to rejoin his corps.

One may imagine the condition of from twelve to fifteen hundred poor wretches clothed in gray great-coats with leaden buttons, shakos shaped like flower-pots, and shoes worn out by marches and counter-marches—pale, weak, most of them without a soù, in a rich city like Leipzig. We did not cut much of a figure among these students, these good citizens and smiling young women, who, despite our glory, looked on us as vagabonds.

All the fine stories of my comrade only made me feel my situation more bitterly.

It is true that we were formerly well received, but in those days our men did not always act honestly by those who treated them like brothers, and now doors were slammed in our faces. We were reduced to the necessity of contemplating squares, churches, and the outside of sausage-shops, which are there very handsome, from morning till night.

We tried every way of amusing ourselves; the idlers played at *drogue*,* the younger ones drank. We had also a game called "Cat and Rat," which

---

* A game at cards, played among soldiers, in which the lose wears a forked stick on his nose till he wins again.

we played in front of the barracks. A stake was planted in the ground, to which two cords were fastened; the rat held one of these, and the cat the other. Their eyes were bandaged. The cat was armed with a cudgel and tried to catch the rat, who kept out of the way as much as he could, listening for the cat's approach—thus they kept going around on tip-toe, and exhibiting their cunning to the company.

Zimmer told me that in former times the good Germans came in crowds to see this game, and you could hear them laugh half a league off when the cat touched the rat with his club. But times were indeed changed; every one passed by now without even turning their heads; we only lost our labor when we tried to interest them in our favor.

During the six weeks we remained at Rosenthal, Zimmer and I often wandered through the city to kill time. We went by way of the faubourg of Randstatt and pushed as far as Lindenau, on the road to Lutzen. There were nothing but bridges, swamps and wooded islets as far as the eye could reach. There we would eat an omelette with bacon at the tavern of the Carp, and wash it down with a bottle of white wine. They no longer gave us credit, as after Jena; I believe, on the contrary, that the innkeeper would have made us pay double and triple, for the honor of the German Fatherland, if my comrade had not known the price of eggs and bacon and wine as well as any Saxon among them.

In the evening, when the sun was setting behind the reeds of the Elster and the Pleisse, we returned to the city accompanied by the mournful notes of the frogs, which swarm in thousands in the marshes.

Sometimes we would stop with folded arms at the railing of a bridge and gaze at the old ramparts of Leipzig, its churches, its old ruins, and its castle of Pleissenbourg, all glowing in the red twilight. The city runs to a point where the Pleisse and the Partha branch off, and the rivers meet above. It is in the shape of a fan, the faubourg of Halle at the handle and the seven other faubourgs spreading off.* We gazed too at the thousand arms of the Elster and the Pleisse, winding like threads among islands already growing dark in

---

* On the English map the river is the Rotha, not the Partha, (or Parde,) and at the point here alluded to it joins the *Elster*, not the *Pleisse*, as stated previously.—*Translator's Note.*

the twilight, although the waters glittered like gold. All this seemed very beautiful.

But if we had known that we would one day be forced to cross these rivers under the enemy's cannon, after having lost the most fearful and the bloodiest of battles, and that entire regiments would disappear beneath those waters, which then gladdened our eyes, I think that the sight would have made us sad enough.

At other times we would walk along the bank of the Pleisse as far as Mark-Kléeberg. It was more than a league, and every field was covered with harvests which they were hastening to garner. The people in their great wagons seemed not to see us, and if we asked for information they pretended not to understand us. Zimmer always grew angry. I held him back, telling him that the beggarly wretches only sought a pretext for falling upon us, and that we had, besides, orders to humor them.

"Very good!" he said; "but if the war comes this way, let them look out! We have overwhelmed them with benefits and this is how they receive us!"

But what shows better yet the ill-feeling of the people toward us was what happened us the day after the conclusion of the armistice, when, about eleven o'clock, we went together to bathe in the Elster. We had already thrown off our clothes, and Zimmer seeing a peasant approaching, cried·

"Holloa, comrade! Is there any danger here?"

"No. Go in boldly," replied the man. "It is a good place."

Zimmer, mistrusting nothing, went some fifteen feet out. He was a good swimmer, but his left arm was yet weak, and the strength of the current carried him away so quickly that he could not even catch the branches of the willows which hung over him; and were it not that he was carried to a ford, where he gained a footing, he would have been swept between two muddy islands, and certainly lost.

The peasant stood to see the effect of his advice. I was very angry, and dressed myself as quickly as I could, shaking my fist at him, but he laughed, and ran, quicker than I could follow him, to the city. Zimmer was wild with wrath, and wished to pursue him to Connewitz; but how could we find him among three or four hundred houses, and if we did find him, what could we do?

Finally we went into the water where there was footing, and its coolness calmed us.

I remember how, as we returned to Leipzig, Zimmer talked of nothing but vengeance.

"The whole country is against us!" cried he; "the citizens look black at us, the women turn their backs, the peasants try to drown us, and the innkeepers refuse us credit, as if we had not conquered them three or four times; and all this comes of our extraordinary goodness; we should have declared that we were their masters! We have granted to the Germans kings and princes; we have even made dukes, counts and barons with the names of their villages; we have loaded them with honors, and see their gratitude!

"Instead of having ordered us to respect the people, we should be given full power over them; then the thieves would change faces and treat us well, as they did in 1806. Force is everything. In the first place, conscripts are made by force, for if they were not forced to come, they would all stay at home. Of the conscripts soldiers are made by force—by discipline being taught them; with soldiers battles are gained by force, and then people are forced to give you everything: they prepare triumphal arches for you and call you heroes because they are afraid of you; that is how it is!"

"But the Emperor is too good. If he were not so good I would not have been in danger of drowning to-day;—the sight of my uniform would have made that peasant tremble at the idea of telling me a lie."

So spoke Zimmer, and all this yet remains in my memory. It happened August 12th, 1813.

Returning to Leipzig, we saw joy painted on the countenances of the inhabitants. It did not display itself openly; but the citizens, meeting, would shake hands with an air of huge satisfaction, and the general rejoicing glistened even in the eyes of servants and the poorest workmen.

Zimmer said: "These Germans seem to be merry about something, they all look so good-natured."

"Yes," I replied; "their good humor comes from the fine weather and good harvest."

It was true the weather was very fine, but when we reached the barracks, we found some of our officers at the gate, talking eagerly together, while those who were going by came up to listen, and then we learned the cause of so much joy. The conference at Prague was broken off, and Austria, too, was about to declare war against us, which gave us two hundred thousand more men to take care of.

I have learned since that we then stood three hundred thousand men against five hundred and twenty thousand, and that among our enemies were two old French generals, Moreau and Bernadotte. Every one can read that in books, but we did not yet know it, and we were sure of victory, for we had never lost a battle. The ill-feeling of the people did not trouble us: in time of war peasants and citizens are in a manner reckoned as nothing; they are only asked for money and provisions, which they always give, for they know that if they made the least resistance they would be stripped to the last farthing.

The day after we got this important news there was a general inspection, and twelve hundred of the wounded of Lutzen were ordered to rejoin their corps. They went by companies with arms and baggage, some following the road to Altenbourg, which runs along the Elster, and some the road to Wurtzen, further to the left.

Zimmer was of the number, having himself asked leave to go. I went with him just beyond the gate, and there we embraced with emotion. I staid behind, as my arm was still weak.

We were now not more than five or six hundred, among whom were a number of masters of arms, of teachers of dancing and French elegance —fellows to be found at all dépôts of wounded. I did not care to become acquainted with them, and my only consolation was in thinking of Catharine, and sometimes of my old comrades Klipfel and Zébédé, of whom I received no tidings.

It was a sad enough life; the people looked upon us with an evil eye; they dared say nothing, knowing that the French army was only four days' march away, and Blücher and Schwartzenberg much further. Otherwise, how soon they would have fallen upon us!

One evening the rumor prevailed that we had just won a great victory at Dresden. There was general consternation; the inhabitants remained shut up in their houses. I went to read the newspaper at the "Bunch of Grapes," in the Rue de Tilly. The French papers were there always on the table; no one opened them but me.

But the following week, at the beginning of September, I saw the same change in people's faces as I observed the day the Austrians declared against us. I guessed we had met some misfortune, and we had, as I learned afterward, for the Paris papers said nothing of it.

Bad weather set in at the end of August, and the rain fell in torrents. I no longer left the barracks. Often, as seated upon my bed, I gazed at the Elster boiling beneath the falling floods, and the trees, and the little islands swaying in the wind, I thought: "Poor soldiers! poor comrades! What are you doing now? Where are you? On the high road perhaps, or in the open fields!"

And despite my sadness at living where I was, I remembered that I was less to be pitied than they. But one day the old Surgeon Tardieu made his round and said to me:

"Your arm is strong again—let us see—raise it for me. All right! all right!"

The next day at roll call, they passed me into a hall where there were clothing, knapsacks, cartridge-boxes and shoes in abundance. I received a musket, two packets of cartridges, and marching papers for the Sixth at Gauernitz, on the Elbe. This was the first of October. Twelve or fifteen of us set out together, under charge of a quartermaster of the Twenty-seventh named Poitevin.

On the road, one after another left us to take the way to his corps; but Poitevin, four infantry men and I, kept on to the village of Gauernitz

XVII.

We were following the Wurtzen high road, our muskets slung on our backs, our great-coat capes turned up, bending beneath our knapsacks, and feeling down-hearted enough, as you may imagine. The rain was falling, and ran from our shakos down our necks; the wind shook the poplars, and their yellow leaves, fluttering around us, told of the approach of winter. So hour after hour passed.

From time to time, at long intervals, we came upon a village with its sheds, dunghills and gardens, surrounded with palings. The women standing behind their windows, with little dull panes, gazed at us as we went by; a dog bayed; a man splitting wood at his threshold turned to follow us with his eyes, and we kept on, on, splashed and muddied to our necks. We looked back; from the end of the village the road stretched on as far as one could see; gray clouds trailed along the despoiled fields, and a few lean rooks were flying away, uttering their melancholy cry.

Nothing could be sadder than such a view; and to it was added the thought that winter was coming on, and that soon we must sleep without a roof, in the snow. We might well be silent, as we were, save the quartermaster Poitevin. He was a veteran,—sallow, wrinkled, with hollow cheeks, moustaches an ell long, and a red nose, like all brandy drinkers. He had a lofty way of speaking, which he interspersed with barrack slang. When the rain came down faster than ever, he cried, with a strange burst of laughter: "Ay, ay, Poitevin, this will teach you to hiss!" The old drunkard perceived that I had a little money in my pocket, and kept near me, saying: "Young man, if your knapsack tires you, hand it to me." But I only thanked him for his kindness.

Notwithstanding my disgust at being with a man who gazed at every tavern sign when we passed through a village, and said at each one: "A little glass of something would do us good, as the time passes," I could not help paying for a glass now and then, so that he did not quit me.

We were nearing Wurtzen and the rain was falling in torrents, when the quartermaster cried for the twentieth time:

"Ay, Poitevin! Here is life for you! This will teach you to hiss!"

"What sort of a proverb is that of yours?" I asked; "I would like to know how the rain would teach you to hiss."

"It is not a proverb, young man; it is an idea which runs in my head when I try to be cheerful."

Then, after a moment's pause, he continued:

"You must know," said he, "that in 1806, when I was a student at Rouen, I happened once to hiss a piece in the theatre, with a number of other young fellows like myself. Some hissed, some applauded; blows were struck, and the police carried us by dozens to the watch-house. The Emperor, hearing of it, said: "Since they like fighting so much, put them in my armies! There they can gratify their tastes!" And, of course, the thing was done; and no one dared hiss in that part of the country, not even fathers and mothers of families."

"You were a conscript, then?" I asked.

"No, my father had just bought me a substitute. It was one of the Emperor's jokes; one of those jokes which we long remember; twenty or thirty of us are dead of hardship and want. A few others, instead of filling honorable positions in their towns, such as doctors, judges, lawyers, have become old drunkards. This is what is called a good joke!"

Then he began to laugh, looking at me from the corner of his eye. I had become very thoughtful, and two or three times more, before we reached Gauernitz, I paid for the poor wretch's little glasses of something.

It was about five o'clock in the evening, and we were approaching the village of Risa, when we descried an old mill, with its wooden bridge, over which a bridle-path ran. We struck off from the road and took this path, to make a short cut to the village, when we heard cries and shrieks for help, and, at the same moment, two women, one old, and the other somewhat younger, ran across a garden, dragging two children with them. They were trying to gain a little wood which bordered the road, and at the same moment we saw several of our soldiers come out of the mill with sacks, while others came up from a cellar with little casks, which they hastened to place on a cart standing near; still others were driving cows and horses from a stable, while an old man stood at the door, with uplifted hands, as if calling down Heaven's curse upon them; and five or six of the evil-minded wretches surrounded the miller, who was all pale, with his eyes starting from their sockets.

The whole scene, the mill, the dam, the broken windows, the flying women, our soldiers in fatigue caps, looking like veritable bandits, the old man cursing them, the cows shaking their heads to throw off those who were leading them, while others pricked them behind with their bayonets—all seems yet before me—I seem yet to see it.

"There," cried the quartermaster, "there are fellows pillaging. We are not far from the army."

"But that is horrible!" I cried. "They are robbers."

"Yes," returned the quartermaster, coolly; "it is contrary to discipline, and if the Emperor knew of it, they would be shot like dogs."

We crossed the little bridge, and found the

thieves crowded around a cask which they had tapped, passing around the cup. This sight roused the quartermaster's indignation, and he cried majestically:

"By whose permission are you plundering in this way?"

Several turned their heads, but seeing that we were but three, for the rest of our party had gone on, one of them replied:

"Ha! what do you want, old joker? A little of the spoil, I suppose. But you need not curl up your moustaches on that account. Here, drink a drop."

The speaker held out the cup, and the quartermaster took it and drank, looking at me as he did so.

"Well, young man," said he, "will you have some, too? It is famous wine, this."

"No, I thank you," I replied.

Several of the pillaging party now cried:

"Hurry, there; it is time to get back to camp."

"No, no," replied others; "there is more to be had here."

"Comrades," said the quartermaster, in a tone of gentle reproof and warning, "you know, comrades, you must go gently about it."

"Yes, yes, old fellow," replied a drum-major, with half-closed eyes, and a mocking smile; "do not be alarmed; we will pluck the pigeon according to rule. We will take care; we will take care."

The quartermaster said no more, but seemed shamed on my account. He at length said:

"What would you have, young man? War is war. One cannot see himself starving, with food at hand."

He was afraid I would report him; he would have remained with the pillagers, but for the fear of being captured. I replied, to relieve his mind:

"Those are probably good fellows, but the sight of a cup of wine makes them forget everything."

At length, about ten o'clock at night, we saw the bivouac fires, on a gloomy hill-side to the right of the village of Gauernitz, and of an old castle from which a few lights also shone. Further on, in the plain, a great number of other fires were burning. The night was clear, and as we approached the bivouac, the sentry challenged:

"Who goes there?"

"France!" replied the quartermaster.

My heart beat, as I thought that, in a few moments, I should again meet my old comrades, if they were yet in the world.

Some men of the guard came forward from a

sort of shed, half a musket-shot from the village, to find out who we were. The commandant of the post, a gray-haired sub-lieutenant, his arm in a sling under his cloak, asked us whence we came, whither we were going, and whether we had met any parties of Cossacks on our route. The quartermaster answered his questions. The lieutenant informed us that Souham's division had that morning left Gauernitz, and ordered us to follow him, that he might examine our marching-papers; which we did in silence, passing among the bivouac fires, around which men, covered with dried mud, were sleeping, in groups of twenty. Not one moved.

We arrived at the officers' quarters. It was an old brick-kiln, with an immense roof, resting on posts driven into the ground. A large fire was burning in it, and the air was agreeably warm. Around it soldiers were sleeping, with a contented look, their backs against the wall; the flames lighted up their figures under the dark rafters. Near the posts shone stacks of arms. I seem yet to see these things; I feel the kindly warmth which penetrated me. I see my comrades, their clothes smoking, a few paces from the kiln, where they were gravely waiting until the officer should have finished reading the marching-papers, by the dim, red light. One bronzed old veteran watched alone, seated on the ground, and mending a shoe with a needle and thread.

The officer handed me back my paper first, saying:

"You will rejoin your battalion to-morrow, two leagues hence, near Torgau."

Then the old soldier, looking at me, placed his hand upon the ground, to show that there was room beside him, and I seated myself. I opened my knapsack, and put on new stockings and shoes, which I had brought from Leipzig, after which I felt much better.

The old man asked:

"You are rejoining your corps?"

"Yes; the Sixth at Torgau."

"And you came from?"——

"The hospital at Leipzig."

"That is easily seen," said he; "you are fat as a beadle. They fed you on chickens down there, while we were eating cow-beef."

I looked around at my sleeping neighbors. He was right; the poor conscripts were mere skin and bone. They were bronzed as veterans, and scarcely seemed able to stand.

The old man, in a moment, continued his questions:

"You were wounded?"

"Yes, veteran, at Lutzen."

"Four months in the hospital!" said he, whistling; "what luck! I have just returned from Spain, flattering myself that I was going to meet the *Kaiserliks* of 1807 once more—sheep, regular sheep—but they have become worse than guerrillas. Everything goes to the bad."

He said the most of this to himself, without paying much attention to me, all the while sewing his shoe, which from time to time he tried on, to be sure that the sewn part would not hurt his foot. At last he put the thread in his knapsack, and the shoe upon his foot, and stretched himself upon a truss of straw.

I was too fatigued to sleep at once, and for an hour lay awake.

In the morning I set out again with the quartermaster Poitevin, and three other soldiers of Souham's division. Our route lay along the bank of the Elbe; the weather was wet and the wind swept fiercely over the river, throwing the spray far on the land.

We hastened on for an hour, when suddenly the quartermaster cried:

"Attention!"

He had halted suddenly, and stood listening. We could hear nothing but the sighing of the of the wind through the trees, and the splash of the waves; but his ear was finer than ours.

"They are skirmishing yonder," said he, pointing to a wood on our right. "The enemy may be near us, and the best thing we can do is to enter the wood and pursue our way cautiously. We can see at the other end of it what is going on; and if the Prussians or Russians are there, we can beat a retreat without their perceiving us. If they are French, we will go on."

We all thought the quartermaster was right; and, in my heart, I admired the shrewdness of the old drunkard. We kept on toward the wood, Poitevin leading, and the others following, with our pieces cocked. We marched slowly, stopping every hundred paces to listen. The shots grew nearer; they were fired at intervals, and the quartermaster said:

"They are sharp-shooters reconnoitering a body of cavalry, for the firing is all on one side."

It was true. In a few moments we perceived, through the trees, a battalion of French infantry, about to make their soup, and in the distance, on the plain beyond, platoons of Cossacks defiling from one village to another. A few skirmishers along the edge of the wood were firing on them, but they were almost beyond musket-range.

"There are your people, young man," said Poitevin. "You are at home."

He had good eyes to read the number of a regiment at such a distance. I could only see ragged soldiers with their cheeks and famine-glistening eyes. Their great-coats were twice too large for them, and fell in folds along their bodies like cloaks. I say nothing of the mud; it was everywhere. No wonder the Germans were exultant, even after our victory at Dresden.

We went toward a couple of little tents, before which three or four horses were nibbling the scanty grass. I saw Colonel Lorain, who now commanded the Third battalion—a tall, thin man, with brown moustaches and a fierce air. He looked at me frowningly, and when I showed my papers, only said:

"Go and rejoin your company."

I started off, thinking that I would recognize some of the Fourth; but, since Lutzen, companies had been so mingled with companies, regiments with regiments, and divisions with divisions, that, on arriving at the camp of the grenadiers, I knew no one. The men seeing me approach, looked distrustfully at me, as if to say:

"Does *he* want some of our beef? Let us see what he brings to the pot!"

I was almost ashamed to ask for my company, when a bony veteran, with a nose long and pointed like an eagle's beak, and a worn-out coat hanging from his shoulders, lifting his head, and gazing at me, said quietly:

"Hold! It is Joseph. I thought he was buried four months ago."

Then I recognized my poor Zébédé. My appearance seemed to affect him, for, without rising, he squeezed my hand, crying:

"Klipfel! here is Joseph!"

Another soldier, seated near a pot, turned his head, saying:

"It is you, Joseph, is it? Then you were not killed."

This was all my welcome. Misery had made them so selfish that they thought only of themselves. But Zébédé was always good-hearted; he made me sit near him, throwing a glance at the others that commanded respect, and offered me his spoon, which he had fastened to the button-hole of his coat. I thanked him, and produced from my knapsack a dozen sausages, a good loaf of bread, and a flask of brandy, which I had the foresight to purchase at Risa. I handed a couple of the sausages to Zébédé, who took them with tears in his eyes. I was also going to offer some to the others; but he put his hand on my arm, saying:

"What is good to eat is good to keep."

We retired from the circle and ate, drinking at the same time; the rest of the soldiers said nothing, but looked wistfully at us. Klipfel, smelling the sausages, turned and said:

"Holloa! Joseph! Come and eat with us. Comrades are always comrades, you know."

"That is all very well," said Zébédé; "but I find meat and drink the best comrades."

He shut up my knapsack himself, saying:

"Keep that, Joseph. I have not been so well regaled for more than a month. You shall not lose by it."

A half-hour after, the recall was beaten; the skirmishers came in, and Sergeant Pinto, who was among the number, recognized me, and said:

"Well; so you have escaped! But you came back in an evil moment! Things go wrong—wrong!"

The colonel and commandants mounted, and we began moving. The Cossacks withdrew. We marched with arms at will; Zébédé was at my side and related all that passed since Lutzen; the great victories of Bautzen and Wurtschen; the forced marches to overtake the retreating enemy; the march on Berlin; then the armistice, during which we were encamped in the little towns; then the arrival of the veterans of Spain —men accustomed to pillaging and living on the peasantry.

Unfortunately, at the close of the armistice all were against us. The country people looked on us with horror; they cut the bridges down, and kept the Russians and Prussians informed of all our movements, and whenever any misfortune happened us, instead of helping us, they tried to force us deeper in the mire. The great rains came to finish us, and the day of the battle of Dresden it fell so heavily that the Emperor's hat hung down upon his shoulders. But when victorious, we only laughed at these things; we felt warm just the same, and we could change our clothes. But the worst of all was when we were beaten, and flying through the mud—hussars, dragoons, and such gentry on our tracks,—we not knowing when we saw a light in the night whether to advance or to perish in the falling deluge.

Zébédé told me all this in detail; how, after the victory of Dresden, General Vandamme, who was to cut off the retreat of the Austrians, had penetrated to Kulm in his ardor; and how those whom we had beaten the day before fell upon him on all sides, front, flank, and rear, and captured him and several other generals, utterly destroying his *corps d'armée*. Two days before, on the 26th of August, a similar misfortune happened to our division, as well as to the Fifth, Sixth, and Eleventh corps on the heights of Lowenberg. We should have crushed the Prussians there, but by a false movement of Marshal Macdonald, the enemy surprised us in a ravine with our artillery in confusion, our cavalry disordered, and our infantry unable to fire owing to the pelting rain; we defended ourselves with the bayonet, and the Third battalion made its way, in spite of the Prussian charges, to the river Katzbach. There Zébédé received two blows on his head from the butt of a grenadier's musket, and was thrown into the river. The current bore him along, while he held Captain Arnauld by the arm; and both would have been lost, if by good luck the captain in the darkness of the night had not seized the overhanging branch of a tree on the other side, and thus managed to regain the bank. He told me how all that night, despite the blood that flowed from his nose and ears, he had marched to the village of Goldberg, almost dead with hunger, fatigue, and his wounds, and how a joiner had taken pity upon him and given him bread, onions, and water. He told me how, on the day following, the whole division, followed by the other corps, had marched across the fields, each one taking his own course, without orders, because the marshals, generals, and all mounted officers had fled as far as possible, in the fear of being captured. He assured me that fifty hussars could have captured them, one after another; but that by good fortune, Blücher could not cross the flooded river, so that they finally rallied at Wolda, where the drummers of every corps beat the march for their regiments at all the corners of the village. By this means every man extricated himself and followed his own drum.

But the happiest thing in this rout was, that a little further on, at Buntzlau, their officers met them, surprised at yet having troops to lead. This was what my comrade told me, to say nothing of the distrust which we were obliged to have of our allies, who at any moment might fall on us unprepared to receive them. He told me how Marshal Oudinot and Marshal Ney had been beaten: the first at Gross-Beeren, and the other at Dennewitz. This was sad indeed, for in these retreats the conscripts died from exhaustion, sickness and every kind of hardship. The veterans of Spain and Germany, hardened by bad weather, could alone resist such fatigue.

"In a word," said Zébédé, "we had everything against us—the country, the continual rains, and our own generals, who were weary of all this. Some of them are dukes and princes, and grow tired of being forever in the mud instead of being seated in comfortable arm-chairs; and others, like Vandamme, are impatient to become Marshals, by performing some grand stroke. We poor wretches, who have nothing to gain but being crippled the the rest of our days, and who are the sons of peasants and workingmen who fought to get rid of one nobility, must perish to create a new one!"

I saw then that the poorest, the most miserable, are not always the most foolish, and that through suffering they come at last to see the sorrowful truth. But I said nothing, and I prayed God to give me strength and courage to support the hardships the coming of which these faults and this injustice foretold.

We were between three armies, who were uniting to crush us; that of the north, commanded by Bernadotte; that of Silesia, commanded by Blücher; and the army of Bohemia, commanded by Schwartzenberg. We believed at one time we were going to cross the Elbe, to fall on the Prussians and Swedes; at another, that we were about attacking the Austrians toward the mountains as we had done fifty times in Italy and other places. But they ended by understanding our movements, and when we seemed to approach, they retired. They feared the Emperor especially, but he could not be at once in Bohemia and Silesia, and so we were forced to make horrible marches and countermarches.

All that the soldiers asked, was to fight, for through marching and sleeping in the mud, half rations and vermin had made their lives a misery. Each one prayed that all this might end one way or the other. It was too much for human endurance; it could not last.

I, myself, at the end of a few days, was weary of such a life; my legs could scarcely support me, and I grew leaner and leaner.

Every night we were disturbed by a beggar, named Thielmann, who raised the peasantry against us; he followed us like a shadow; watched us from village to village, on the heights, on the roads, in the valleys; his army were all who bore us a grudge, and he had always men enough.

It was about this time, too, that the Bavarians, the Badeners and the Wurtembergers declared against us, so that all Europe was upon us.

At length we had the consolation of seeing that the army was collecting as for a great battle; instead of meeting Platow's Cossacks and Thielmann's partisans in the neighborhood of villages, we found hussars, chasseurs, dragoons from Spain, artillery, pontoon trains on the march. The rain still fell in floods; those who could no longer drag themselves along sat down in the mud at the foot of a tree and abandoned themselves to their unhappy fate.

The eleventh of October we bivouacked near the village of Lousig; the twelfth near Graffen heinichen; the thirteenth we crossed the Mulda and saw the Old Guard defile across the bridge, and La-Tour-Maubourg. It was announced that the Emperor crossed too, but we departed with Dombrowski's division and Souham's corps.

At moments the rain would cease falling and a ray of autumn sun shine out from between the clouds, and then we could see the whole army marching; cavalry and infantry advancing from all sides, on Leipzig. On the other side of the Mulda glittered the bayonets of the Prussians; but we yet saw no Austrians and Russians: they doubtless came from other directions.

On the fourteenth of October, our battalion was detached to reconnoitre the village of Aaken. The enemy were in force there, and received us with a scattering artillery fire, and we remained all night without being able to light a fire, on account of the pouring rain. The next day we set out to rejoin our division by forced marches. Every one said, I know not why:

"The battle is approaching! the fight is coming on!"

Sergeant Pinto declared that he felt the Emperor in the air. I felt nothing, but I knew that we were marching on Leipzig, and I thought to myself, "If we have a battle, God grant that you do not get an ugly hurt as at Lutzen, and that you may see Catharine again!" The night following the weather cleared up a little, thousands of stars shone out, and we still kept on. The next day, about ten o'clock, near a village whose name I cannot recollect, we were ordered to halt, and then we felt a trembling in the air. The colonel and Sergeant Pinto said:

"The battle has begun!" and at the same moment, the colonel, waving his sword, cried:

"Forward!"

We started at a run; knapsacks, cartouche-boxes muskets, mud, all drove on; we cared for nothing. Half an hour after we saw, a few thousand paces ahead, a long column, in which followed artillery, cavalry, and infantry, one after the other; behind us, on the road to Duben, we saw another, all pushing forward at their utmost speed. Regiments even advancing at the double quick across the fields.

At the end of the road we could see the two spires of the churches of Saint Nicholas and Saint Thomas in Leipzig, piercing the sky, while to the right and left, on both sides of the city, rose great clouds of smoke through which broad flashes were darting. The noise increased; we were yet more than a league from the city, but we were forced to almost shout to hear each other, and men gazed around, pale as death, seeming by their looks to say:

"This is indeed a battle?"

Sergeant Pinto cried that it was worse than Eylau. He laughed no more, nor did Zébédé; but on, on we rushed, officers incessantly urging us forward. We seemed to grow delirious; the love of country was indeed striving within us, but still greater was the furious eagerness for the fight.

At eleven o'clock, we descried the battle-field about a league in front of Leipzig. We saw the steeples and roofs crowded with people, and the old ramparts on which I had walked so often, thinking of Catharine. Opposite us, twelve or fifteen hundred yards distant, two regiments of red lancers were drawn up, and a little to the left, two or three regiments of mounted chasseurs in the fields along the Partha, and between them filed the long column from Duben. Further on, along the slope, were the divisions Ricard, Dombrowski, Souham, and several others, with their rear to the city; cannons limbered, with their caissons—the cannoneers and artillerymen on horseback—stood ready to start off; and far behind, on a hill, around one of those old farm-houses with flat roofs and immense outlying sheds, so often seen in that country, glittered the brilliant uniforms of the staff.

It was the army of reserve, commanded by Ney. His left wing communicated with Marmont, who was posted on the road to Halle, and his right with the grand army, commanded by the Emperor in person. In this manner our troops formed an immense circle around Leipzig: and the enemy, arriving from all points, sought to join their divisions so as to form a yet larger circle around us, and to inclose us in Leipzig as in a trap.

While we waited thus, three fearful battles were going on at once: one against the Austrians and Russians at Wachau; another against the Prussians at Mockern on the road to Halle; and the third on the road to Lutzen, to defend the bridge of Lindenau, attacked by General Giulay.

These things I learned afterwards; but every one ought to tell what he saw himself: in this way the world will know the truth.

XVIII

The battalion was commencing to descend the hill, opposite Leipzig, to rejoin our division, when we saw a staff-officer crossing the plain below, and coming at full gallop toward us. In two minutes he was with us; Colonel Lorain had spurred forward to meet him; they exchanged a few words, and the officer returned. Hundreds of others were rushing over the plain in the same manner, bearing orders.

"Head of column to the right!" shouted the colonel.

We took the direction of a wood, which skirts the Duben road some half a league. It was a beech forest, but in it were birches and oaks. Once at its borders, we were ordered to re-prime our guns, and the battalion was deployed through the wood as skirmishers. We advanced twenty-five paces apart, and each of us kept his eyes well opened, as may be imagined. Every minute Sergeant Pinto would cry out:

"Get under cover!"

But he did not need to warn us: each one hastened to take his post behind a stout tree, to reconnoitre well before proceeding to another. To what dangers must peaceable people be exposed! We kept on in this manner some ten minutes, and, as we saw nothing, began to grow confident, when suddenly, one, two, three shots rang out. Then they came from all sides, and rattled from end to end of our line. At the same instant I saw my comrade on the left fall, trying, as he sank to the earth, to support himself by the trunk of the tree behind which he was standing. This roused me. I looked to the right and saw, fifty or sixty paces off, an old Prussian soldier, with his long red moustaches covering the lock of his piece; he was aiming deliberately at me. I fell at once to the ground, and at the same moment heard the report. It was a close escape, for the comb, brush, and handkerchief in my shako were broken and torn by the bullet. A cold shiver ran through me.

"Well done! a miss is as good as a mile!"

cried the old sergeant, starting forward at a run, and I, who had no wish to remain longer in such a place, followed with right good-will.

Lieutenant Bretonville, waving his sabre, cried, "Forward!" while, to the right, the firing still continued. We soon arrived at a clearing, where lay five or six trunks of felled trees, and a little lake full of high grass, but not a tree standing, that might serve us for a cover. Nevertheless, five or six of our men advanced boldly, when the sergeant called out:

"Halt! The Prussians are in ambush around us. Look sharp!"

Scarcely had he spoken, when a dozen bullets whistled through the branches, and at the same time, a number of Prussians rose, and plunged deeper into the forest opposite.

"There they go! Forward!" cried Pinto.

But the bullet in my shako had rendered me cautious; it seemed as if I could almost see through the trees, and, as the sergeant started forth into the clearing, I held his arm, pointing out to him the muzzle of a musket peeping out from a bush, not a hundred paces before us. The others, clustering around, saw it too, and Pinto whispered:

"A DOZEN BULLETS WHISTLED THROUGH THE BRANCHES." (Page 271.)

"Stay, Bertha; remain here and do not lose sight of him, while we turn the position."

They set off, to the right and left, and I, behind my tree, my piece at my shoulder, waited like a hunter for his game. At the end of two or three minutes, the Prussian, hearing nothing, rose slowly. He was quite a boy, with little blonde moustaches, and a tall, slight, but well-knit figure. I could have killed him as he stood, but the thought of thus slaying a defenceless man froze my blood. Suddenly he saw me, and bounded aside. Then I fired, and breathed more freely as I saw him running, like a stag, toward the wood.

At the same moment, five or six reports rang out to the right and left: the sergeant, Zébédé, Klipfel, and the rest appeared, and a hundred paces further on we found the young Prussian upon the ground, blood gushing from his mouth. He gazed at us with a scared expression, raising his arms, as if to parry bayonet-thrusts, but the sergeant called gleefully to him:

"Fear nothing! Your account is settled."

No one offered to injure him further; but Klipfel took a beautiful pipe, which was hanging out of his pocket, saying:

"For a long time I have wanted a pipe, and here is a fine one."

"Fusiler Klipfel!" cried Pinto, indignantly, "will you be good enough to put back that pipe? Leave it to the Cossacks to rob the wounded! A French soldier knows only honor!"

Klipfel threw down the pipe and we departed, not one caring to look back at the wounded Prussian. We arrived at the edge of the forest, outside which, among tufted bushes, the Prussians we pursued had taken refuge. We saw them rise to fire upon us, but they immediately lay down again. We might have remained there tranquilly, since we had orders to occupy the wood, and the shots of the Prussians could not hurt us, protected as we were by the trees. On the other side of the slope we heard a terrific battle going on; the thunder of cannon was increasing, it filled the air with one continuous roar. But our officers held a council, and decided that the bushes were a part of the forest, and that the Prussians must be driven from them. This determination cost many a life.

We received orders, then, to drive the enemy's tirailleurs, and as they fired as we came on, we started at a run, so as to be upon them before they could reload. Our officers ran, also full of ardor. We thought the bushes ended at the top of the hill, and that we could sweep off the Prussians by dozens. But scarcely had we arrived, out of breath, upon the ridge, when old Pinto cried:

"Hussars!"

I looked up, and saw the *Colbacks* rushing down upon us like a tempest. Scarcely had I seen them, when I began to spring down the hill, going, I verily believe, in spite of weariness and my knapsack, fifteen feet at a bound. I saw before me, Pinto, Zébédé, and the others, making their best speed. Behind, on came the hussars, their officers shouting orders in German, their scabbards clanking and horses neighing. The earth shook beneath them.

I took the shortest road to the wood, and had almost reached it, when I came upon one of the trenches where the peasants were in the habit of digging clay for their houses. It was more than twenty feet wide, and forty or fifty long, and the rain had made the sides very slippery; but as I heard the very breathing of the horses behind me, while my hair rose on my head, without thinking of aught else, I sprang forward, and fell upon my face: another fusilier of my company was already there. We rose as soon as we could, and at the same instant two hussars glided down the slippery side of the trench. The first, cursing like a fiend, aimed a sabre-stroke at my poor comrade's head, but as he rose in his stirrups to give force to the blow I buried my bayonet in his side, while the other brought down his blade upon my shoulder with such force, that, were it not for my epaulette, I believe that I had been well-nigh cloven in two. Then he lunged, but as the point of his sabre touched my breast, a bullet from above crashed through his skull. I looked around, and saw one of our men, up to his knees in the clay. He had heard the oaths of the hussars and the neighing of the horses, and had come to the edge of the trench to see what was going on.

"Well, comrade," said he, laughing, "it was about time."

I had not strength to reply, but stood trembling like an aspen leaf. He unfixed his bayonet, and stretched the muzzle of his piece to me to help me out. Then I squeezed his hand, saying:

"You saved my life! What is your name?"

He told me that his name was Jean Pierre Vincent. I have often since thought that I should be only too happy to render that man any service in my power; but two days after, the second battle of Leipzig took place; then the retreat from Hanau began, and I never saw him again.

Sergeant Pinto and Zébédé came up a moment after. Zébédé said:

"We have escaped once more, Joseph, and now we are the only Phalsbourg men in the battalion. Klipfel was sabred by the hussars."

"Did you see him?" I cried.

"Yes; he received over twenty wounds, and kept calling to me for aid." Then, after a moment's pause, he added, "O Joseph! it is terrible to hear the companion of your childhood calling for help, and not be able to give it! But they were too many. They surrounded him on all sides."

The thoughts of home rushed upon both our minds. I thought I could see grandmother Klipfel when she would learn the news, and this made me think too of Catharine.

From the time of the charge of the hussars until night, the battalion remained in the same position, skirmishing with the Prussians. We kept them from occupying the wood; but they prevented us from ascending to the ridge. The next day we knew why. The hill commanded the entire course of the Partha, and the fierce cannonade we heard came from Dombrowski's division, which was attacking the Prussian left wing, in order to aid General Marmont at Mockern, where twenty thousand French, posted in a ravine, were holding eighty thousand of Blücher's troops in check; while toward Wachau a hundred and fifteen thousand French were engaged with two hundred thousand Austrians and Russians. More than fifteen hundred cannon were thundering at once. Our poor little fusilade was like the humming of a bee in a storm, and we sometimes ceased firing, on both sides, to listen. It seemed as if some supernatural, infernal battle were going on; the air was filled with smoke; the earth trembled beneath our feet: old soldiers like Pinto declared they had never seen anything like it.

About six o'clock, a staff-officer brought orders to Colonel Lorain, and immediately after a retreat was sounded. The battalion had lost sixty men by the charge of Russian hussars and the musketry.

It was night when we left the forest, and on

the banks of the Partha—among caissons, wagons, retreating divisions, ambulances filled with wounded, all defiling over the two bridges—we had to wait more than two hours for our turn to cross. The heavens were black; the artillery still growled afar off, but the three battles were ended. We heard that we had beaten the Austrians and the Russians at Wachau, on the other side of Leipzig; but our men returning from Mockern were downcast and gloomy; not a voice cried *Vive l'Empereur!* as after a victory.

Once on the other side of the river, the battalion proceeded down the Partha a good half-league, as far as the village of Schœnfeld; the night was damp; we marched along heavily, our muskets on our shoulders, our heads bent down, and our eyes closing for want of sleep.

Behind us the great column of cannon, caissons, baggage-wagons and troops retreating from Mockern filled the air with a hoarse murmur, and from time to time the cries of the artillerymen and teamsters, shouting to make room, arose above the tumult. But these noises insensibly grew less, and we at length reached a burial-ground, where we were ordered to stack arms and break ranks.

By this time the sky had cleared, and I recognized Schœnfeld in the moonlight. How often had I eaten bread and drank white wine with Zimmer there at the Golden Sheaf, when the sun shone brightly and the leaves were green around! But those times had passed!

Sentries were posted, and a few men went to the village for wood and provisions. I sat against the cemetery wall, and at length fell asleep. About three o'clock in the morning, I was awoke.

It was Zébédé. "Joseph," said he, "come to the fire. If you remain here, you run the risk of catching the fever."

I arose, sick with fatigue and suffering. A fine rain filled the air. My comrade drew me toward the fire, which smoked in the drizzling atmosphere; it seemed to give out no heat; but Zébédé having made me drink a draught of brandy I felt at least less cold, and gazed at the bivouac fires on the other side of the Partha.

"The Prussians are warming themselves in our wood," said Zébéde.

"Yes," I replied; "and poor Klipfel is there too, but he no longer feels the cold."

My teeth chattered. These words saddened us both. A few moments after Zébédé resumed:

"Do you remember, Joseph, the black ribbon he wore the day of the conscription, and how he cried, 'We are all condemned to death, like those gone to Russia? I want a black ribbon. We must wear our own mourning!' And his little brother said: No, no, Jacob, I do not want it!' and wept; but Klipfel put on the black ribbon notwithstanding; he saw the hussars in his dreams."

As Zébédé spoke, I recalled those things, and I saw too that wretch Pinacle on the Town Hall Square, calling me and shaking a black ribbon over his head: "Ha, cripple! you must have a fine ribbon; the ribbon of those who win!"

This remembrance, together with the cold, which seemed to freeze the very marrow in our bones, made me shudder. I thought Pinacle was right; that I had seen the last of home. I thought of Catharine, of Aunt Grédel, of good Monsieur Goulden, and I cursed those who had forced me from them.

At daybreak, wagons arrived with food and brandy for us. The rain had ceased; we made soup, but nothing could warm me; I had caught the fever; within I was cold while my body burned. I was not the only one in the battalion in that condition; three fourths of the men were suffering from it; and, for a month before, those who could no longer march had lain down by the roadside weeping and calling upon their mothers like little children. Hunger, forced marches, the rain, and grief had done their work, and happy was it for the parents that they could not see their cherished sons perishing along the road; it would be too fearful; many would think there was no mercy in earth or heaven.

As the light increased, we saw to the left, on the other side of the river—and of a great ravine filled with willows and aspens—burnt villages, heaps of dead, abandoned wagons, broken caissons, dismounted cannon and ravaged fields stretched as far as the eye could reach on the Halle, Lindenthal and Dölitch roads. It was worse than at Lutzen. We saw the Prussians deploy, and advance their thousands over the battle-field. They were to join with the Russians and Austrians and close the great circle around us, and we could not prevent them, especially as Bernadotte and the Russian General Beningsen had come up with twenty thousand fresh troops. Thus, after fighting three battles in one day, were we, only one hundred and thirty thousand strong, seemingly about to be entrapped in the midst of three hundred thousand bayonets, not to speak of fifty thousand horse and twelve hundred cannon.

From Schoenfeld, the battalion started to rejoin the division at Kohlgarten. All the roads were lined with slow-moving ambulances, filled with wounded; all the wagons of the country around had been impressed for this service; and, in the intervals between them, marched hundreds of poor fellows with their arms in slings, or their heads bandaged—pale, crestfallen, half dead. All who could drag themselves along kept out of the ambulances, but tried nevertheless to reach a hospital. We made our way, with a thousand difficulties, through this mass, when, near Kohlgarten, twenty hussars, galloping at full speed, and with levelled pistols, drove back the crowd, right and left, into the fields, shouting, as they pressed on;

'The Emperor! the Emperor!"

The battalion drew up, and presented arms; and a few moments after, the mounted grenadiers of the guard—veritable giants, with their great boots, their immense bear-skin hats, descending to their shoulders and only allowing their moustaches, nose, and eyes to remain visible—passed at a gallop. Our men looked joyfully at them, glad that such robust warriors were on our side.

Scarcely had they passed, when the staff tore after. Imagine a hundred and fifty to two hundred marshals, generals, and other superior officers, mounted on magnificent steeds, and so covered with embroidery that the color of their uniforms was scarcely visible; some tall, thin, and haughty; others short, thick-set, and red-faced; others again young and handsome, sitting like statues in their saddles; all with eager look and flashing eyes. It was a magnificent and terrible sight.

But the most striking figure among those captains, who for twenty years had made Europe tremble, was Napoleon himself, with his old hat and gray overcoat; his large, determined chin and neck buried between his shoulders. All shouted, "*Vive l'Empereur!*" but he heard nothing of it. He paid no more attention to us than to the drizzling rain which filled the air, but gazed with contracted brows at the Prussian army stretching along the Partha to join the Austrians. So I saw him on that day and so he remains in my memory. The battalion had been on the march for a quarter of an hour, when at length Zébédé said:

"Did you see him, Joseph?"

"I did," I replied; "I saw him well, and I will remember the sight all my life."

"It is strange," said my comrade: "he does not seem to be pleased. At Wurschen, the day after the battle, he seemed rejoiced to hear our '*Vive l'Empereur!*' and the generals all wore merry faces too. To-day they seem savage, and nevertheless the captain said that we bore off the victory on the other side of Leipzig."

Others thought the same thing without speaking of it, but there was a growing uneasiness among all.

We found the regiment bivouacked near Kohlgarten. In every direction camp-fires were rolling their smoke to the sky. A drizzling rain continued to fall, and the men, seated on their knapsacks around the fires, seemed depressed and gloomy. The officers formed groups of their own. On all sides it was whispered that such a war had never before been seen; it was one of extermination; that it did not help us to defeat the enemy, for they only desired to kill us off, knowing that they had four or five times our number of men, and would finally remain masters.

They said, too, that the Emperor had won the battle at Wachau, against the Austrians and

Russians; but that the victory was useless, because they did not retreat, but stood awaiting masses of reinforcements. On the side of Mockern we knew that we had lost, in spite of Marmont's splendid defence; the enemy had crushed us beneath the weight of their numbers. We only had one real advantage that day on our side; that was keeping our line of retreat on Erfurt: for Giulay had not been able to seize the bridges of the Elster and Pleisse. All the army, from the simple soldier to the marshal, thought that we would have to retreat as soon as possible, and that our position was of the worst; unfortunately the Emperor thought otherwise, and we had to remain.

All day on the seventeenth we lay in our position without firing a shot. A few spoke of the arrival of General Regnier with sixteen thousand Saxons; but the defection of the Bavarians taught us what confidence we could put in our allies.

Toward evening of the next day, we discovered the army of the north on the plateau of Breitenfeld. This was sixty thousand more men for the enemy. I can yet hear the maledictions levelled at Bernadotte—the cries of indignation of those who knew him as a simple officer in the army of the Republic, who cried out that he owed us all

—that we made him a king with our blood, and that he now came to give us the finishing blow.

That night, a general movement rearward was made; our lines drew closer and closer around Leipzig; then all became quiet. But this did not prevent our reflecting; on the contrary, every one thought, in the silence:

"What will to-morrow bring forth? Shall I at this hour see the moon rising among the clouds as I now see her? Will the stars yet shine for me to see?"

And when, in the dim night, we gazed at the circle of fire which for nearly six leagues stretched around us, we cried within ourselves:

"Now indeed the world is against us; all nations demand our extermination; they want no more of our glory!"

But we remembered that we had the honor of bearing the name of Frenchmen, and must conquer or die.

XIX.

IN the midst of such thoughts, day broke. Nothing was stirring yet, and Zébédé said:

"What a chance for us, if the enemy should fear to attack us!"

The officers spoke of an armistice; but suddenly about nine o'clock, our couriers came galloping in, crying that the enemy was moving his whole line down upon us, and directly after we heard cannon on our right, along the Elster. We were already under arms, and set out across the fields toward the Partha to return to Schoenfeld. The battle had begun.

On the hills overlooking the river, two or three divisions, with batteries in the intervals, and cannon at the flanks, awaited the enemy's approach; beyond, over the points of their bayonets, we could see the Prussians, the Swedes, and the Russians, advancing on all sides in deep, never-ending masses. Shortly after, we took our place in line, between two hills, and then we saw five or six thousand Prussians crossing the river, and all together shouting, "*Vaterland! Vaterland!*" This caused a tremendous tumult, like that of clouds of rooks flying north.

At the same instant the musketry opened from both sides of the river. The valley through which the Partha flows was filled with smoke; the Prussians were already upon us—we could see their furious eyes and wild looks; they seemed like savage beasts rushing down on us. Then but one shout of "*Vive l'Empereur!*" smote the sky and we dashed forward. The shock was terrible; thousands of bayonets crossed; we drove them back, were ourselves driven back; muskets were clubbed; the opposing ranks were confounded and mingled in one mass; the fallen were trampled upon, while the thunder of artillery, the whistling of bullets, and the thick white smoke inclosing all, made the valley seem the pit of hell, peopled by contending demons.

Despair urged us, and the wish to revenge our deaths before yielding up our lives. The pride of boasting that they once defeated Napoleon incited the Prussians; for they are the proudest of men, and their victories at Gross-Beeren and Katzbach had made them fools. But the river swept away them and their pride! Three times they crossed and rushed at us. We were indeed forced back by the shock of their numbers, and how they shouted then! They seemed to wish to devour us. Their officers, waving their swords in the air, cried, "*Vorwärtz! Vorwärtz!*" and all advanced like a wall, with the greatest courage—that we cannot deny. Our cannon opened huge gaps in their lines; still they pressed on; but at the top of the hill we charged again, and drove them to the river. We would have massacred them to a man, were it not for one of their batteries before Mockern, which enfiladed us and forced us to give up the pursuit.

This lasted until two o'clock; half our officers were killed or wounded; the Colonel, Lorain, was among the first, and the Commandant, Gémeau, the latter; all along the river side were heaps of dead, or wounded men crawling away from the struggle. Some, furious, would rise to their knees to fire a last shot or deliver a final bayonet-thrust. Never was anything seen like it. In the river floated long lines of corpses, some showing their faces, others their backs, others their feet. They followed each other like rafts of wood, and no one paid the least attention to the sight—no one of us knew that the same might not be his condition at any minute.

The carnage reached from Schoenfeld to Grossdorf, along the Partha.

At length the Swedes and Prussians ceased their attacks, and started farther up the river to turn our position, and masses of Russians came to occupy the places they had left.

The Russians formed in two columns, and descended to the valley, with shouldered arms, in admirable order. Twice they assailed us with the greatest bravery, but without uttering wild beasts' cries, like the Prussians. Their cavalry attempted to carry the old bridge above Schoenfeld, and the cannonade increased. On all sides, as far as eye could reach, we saw only the enemy massing their forces, and when we had repulsed one of their columns, another of fresh men took its place. The fight had ever to be fought over again.

Between two and three o'clock, we learned that the Swedes and the Prussian cavalry had crossed the river above Grossdorf, and were about to take us in the rear, a mode which pleased them much better than fighting face to face. Marshal Ney immediately changed front, throwing his right wing to the rear. Our division still remained supported on Schoenfeld, but all the others retired from the Partha, to stretch along the plain, and the entire army formed but one line around Leipzig.

The Russians, behind the road to Mockern, prepared for a third attack toward three o'clock; our officers were making new dispositions to receive them; when a sort of shudder ran from one end of our lines to the other, and in a few moments all knew that the sixteen thousand Saxons and the Wurtemberg cavalry, in our very centre, had passed over to the enemy, and that on their way they had the infamy to turn the forty guns they carried with them, on their old brother-in-arms of Durutte's division.

This treason, instead of discouraging us, so added to our fury, that if we had been allowed, we would have crossed the river to massacre them. They say that they were defending their country. It is false! They had only to have left us on the Duben road; why did they not go then? They might have done like the Bavarians and quitted us before the battle; they might have remained neutral—might have refused to serve; but they deserted us only because fortune was against us. If they knew we were going to win, they would have continued our very good friends, so that they might have their share of the spoil or glory—as after Jena and Friedland. This is what every one thought, and it is why those Saxons are, and will ever remain, traitors: not only did they abandon their friends in distress, but they murdered them, to make a welcome with the enemy. God is just, and so great was their new allies' scorn of them, that they divided half Saxony between themselves after the battle. The French might well laugh at Prussian, Austrian, and Russian gratitude.

From the time of this desertion until evening, it was a war of vengeance that we carried on; the allies might crush us by numbers, but they should pay dearly for their victory!

At nightfall, while two thousand pieces of artillery were thundering together, we were attacked for the seventh time in Schoenfeld. The Russians on one side and the Prussians on the other poured in upon us. We defended every house. In every lane the walls crumbled beneath the bullets, and roofs fell in on every side. There were now no shouts as at the beginning of the battle; all were cool and pale with rage. The officers had collected scattered muskets and cartridge-boxes, and now loaded and fired like the men. We defended the gardens, too, and the cemetery, where we had bivouacked, until there were more dead above than beneath the soil. Every inch of earth cost a life.

It was night when Marshal Ney brought up a reinforcement—whence I knew not. It was what remained of Ricard's division and Souham's Second. The *débris* of our regiments united, and hurled the Russians to the other side of the old bridge, which no longer had a rail, that having been swept away by the shot. Six twelve-pounders were posted on the bridge and maintained a fire for one hour longer. The remainder of the battalion, and of some others in our rear, supported the guns; and I remember how their flashes lit up the forms of men and horses, heaped beneath the dark arches. The sight lasted only a moment, but it was a horrible moment indeed!

At half-past seven, masses of cavalry advanced on our left, and we saw them whirling about two large squares, which slowly retired. Then we received orders to retreat. Not more than two or there thousand men remained at Schoenfeld with the six pieces of artillery. We reached Kohlgarten without being pursued, and were to bivouac around Rendnitz. Zébédé was yet living, and, as we marched on, listening to the cannonade, which continued, despite the darkness, along the Elster, he said, suddenly:

"How is it that we are here, Joseph, when so many thousand others that stood by our side are dead? It seems as if we bore charmed lives, and could not die."

I made no reply.

"Think you there was ever before such a battle?" he asked. "No, it cannot be. It is impossible."

It was indeed a battle of giants. From ten in the morning until seven in the evening, we had held our own against three hundred and sixty thousand men, without, at night, having lost an inch: and, nevertheless, we were but a hundred and thirty thousand. God keep me from speaking ill of the Germans. They were fighting for the independence of their country. But they might do better than celebrate the anniversary of the battle of Leipzig every year. There is not much to boast of in fighting an enemy three to one.

Approaching Rendnitz, we marched over heaps of dead. At every step we encountered dismounted cannon, broken caissons, and trees cut down by shot. There a division of the Young Guard and the mounted grenadiers, led by Napoleon himself, had repulsed the Swedes who were advancing into the breach made by the treachery of the Saxons. Two or three burning houses lit up the scene. The mounted grenadiers were yet at Rendnitz, but crowds of disbanded troops were passing up and down the street. No rations had been distributed, and all were seeking something to eat and drink.

As we defiled by a large house, we saw behind the wall of a court two *cantinières*, who were giving the soldiers drink from their wagons. There were there chasseurs, cuirassiers, lancers, hussars, infantry of the line and of the guard, all mingled together, with torn uniforms, broken shakos, and plumeless helmets, and all seemingly famished.

Two or three dragoons stood on the wall, near a pot of burning pitch, their arms crossed on their long white cloaks, covered from head to foot with blood, like butchers.

Zébédé, without speaking, pushed me with

his elbow, and we entered the court, while the others pursued their way. It took us full a quarter of an hour to reach one of the wagons. I held up a crown of six livres, and the *cantinière*, kneeling behind her cask, handed me a large glass of brandy and a piece of white bread, at the same time taking my money. I drank and passed the glass to Zébédé, who emptied it. We had as much difficulty in getting out of the crowd as in entering. Hard, famished faces and cavernous eyes were on all sides of us. No one moved willingly. Each thought only of himself, and cared not for his neighbor. They had escaped a thousand deaths to-day only to dare a thousand more to-morrow. Well might they mutter, "Every one for himself, and God for us all."

As we went through the village street, Zébédé said, "You have bread?"

"Yes."

I broke it in two, and gave him half. We began to eat, at the same time hastening on. We heard distant firing. At the end of twenty minutes we had overtaken the rear of the column, and recognized the battalion of Captain Adjutant-Major Vidal, who was marching near it. We had taken our places in the ranks before any one noticed our absence.

The nearer we approached the city the more detachments, cannon and baggage we encountered hastening to Leipzig.

Toward ten o'clock we passed through the faubourg of Rendnitz. The general of brigade, Fournier, took command of us and ordered us to oblique to the left. At midnight we arrived at the long promenades which border the Pleisse, and halted under the old leafless lindens, and stacked arms. A long line of fires flickered in the fog as far as Randstadt; and, when the flames burnt high, they threw a glare on groups of Polish lancers, lines of horses, cannon, and wagons, while, at intervals beyond, sentinels stood like statues in the mist. A heavy, hollow sound arose from the city, and mingled with the rolling of our trains over the bridge at Lindenau. It was the beginning of the retreat.

Then every one put his knapsack at the foot of a tree and stretched himself on the ground, his arm under his head. A quarter of an hour after all were sleeping.

XX.

WHAT occurred until daybreak I know not. Baggage, wounded, and prisoners doubtless continued to crowd across the bridge. But then a a terrific shock woke us all. We started up, thinking the enemy were upon us, when two officers of hussars came galloping in with the news that a powder wagon had exploded by accident in the grand avenue of Randstadt, at the river-side. The dark, red smoke rolled up to the sky, and slowly disappeared, while the old houses continued to shake as if an earthquake were rolling by.

Quiet was soon restored. Some lay down to sleep: but it was growing lighter every minute; and, glancing toward the river, I saw our troops extending until lost in the distance along the five bridges of the Elster and Pleisse, which follow one after another, and make, so to speak, but one. Thousands of men must defile over this bridge, and, of necessity, take time in doing so. And the idea struck every one that it would have been much better to have thrown several bridges across the two rivers; for at any instant the enemy might attack us, and then retreat would have become difficult indeed. But the Emperor had forgotten to give the order, and no one dared do anything without orders. Not a marshal of France would have dared to take it upon himself to say that two bridges were better than one. To such a point had the terrible discipline of Napoleon reduced those old captains! They obeyed like machines, and disturbed themselves about nothing. Such was their fear of displeasing their master.

As I gazed at that bridge, which seemed endless, I thought, "Heaven grant that they may let us cross now, for we have had enough of battles and carnage! Once on the other side and we are on the road to France, indeed, and I may again see Catharine, Aunt Grédel, and Father Goulden!" So thinking, I grew sad; I gazed at the thousands of artillerymen and baggage-guards swarming over the bridge, and saw the tall bear-skin shakos of the Old Guard, who stood with shouldered arms immovable on the hill of Lindenau on the other side of the river — and as I thought they were fairly on their way to France, how I longed to be in their place! Zébédé, through whose mind the same thoughts were running, said:

"Hey! Joseph; if we were only there!"

But I felt bitterly, indeed, when, about seven o'clock, three wagons came to distribute provisions and ammunition among us, and it became evident that we were to become the rear-guard. In spite of my hunger, I felt like throwing my bread against a wall. A few moments after, two squadrons of Polish lancers appeared coming up the bank, and behind them five or six generals, Poniatowski among the number. He was a man of about fifty, tall, slight, and with a melancholy expression. He passed without looking at us. General Fournier, who now commanded our brigade, spurred from among his staff, and cried:

"By file, left!"

I never so felt my heart sink. I would have sold my life for two farthings; but nevertheless, we had to move on, and turn our backs to the bridge.

We soon arrived at a place called Hinterthor—an old gate on the road to Caunewitz. To the right and left stretched ancient ramparts, and behind, rows of houses. We were posted in covered roads, near this gate, which the sappers had strongly barricaded. Captain Vidal then commanded the battalion, reduced to three hundred and twenty-five men. A few worm-eaten palisades served us for intrenchments, and, on all the roads before us, the enemy were advancing. This time they wore white coats and flat caps, with a raised piece in front, on which we could see the two-headed eagle of the *kreutzers*. Old Pinto, who recognized them at once, cried:

"Those fellows are the *kaiserliks!* We have beaten them fifty times since 1793; but if the father of Marie Louise had a heart, they would be with us now instead of against us."

For some moments a cannonade had been going on at the other side of the city, where Blücher was attacking the faubourg of Halle.

Soon after, the firing stretched along to the right; it was Bernadotte attacking the faubourg of Kohlgartenthor, and at the same time the first shells of the Austrians fell in our covered ways; they followed in file; many passing over

Hinterthor, burst in the houses and the streets of the faubourg.

At nine o'clock the Austrians formed their columns of attack on the Caunewitz road, and poured down on us from all sides. Nevertheless we held our own until about ten o'clock, and then were forced back to the old ramparts, through the breaches of which the Kaiserliks pursued us under the cross-fire of the Fourteenth and Twenty-ninth of the line. The poor Austrians were not inspired with the fury of the Prussians, but nevertheless, showed a true courage; for, at half past ten they had won the ramparts, and although, from all the neighboring windows, we kept up a deadly fire, we could not force them back. Six months before it would have horrified me to think of men being thus slaughtered, but now I was as insensible as any old soldier, and the death of one man or of a hundred would not cost me a thought.

Until this time all had gone well, but how were we to get out of the houses? Unless we climbed on the roof, retreat was no longer possible. This again was one of those terrible moments I shall never forget. All at once the idea struck me that we should be caught like foxes which

they smoke in their holes. The enemy held every
avenue. I went to a window in the rear, and saw
that it looked out on a yard, and that the yard
had no gate except in front. I thought it not un-
likely that the Austrians, in revenge for the loss
we had inflicted upon them, might put us to the point
of the bayonet. It would have been natural enough.
Thinking thus, I ran back to a room, where a
dozen of us yet remained, and there I saw Sergeant Pinto leaning against the wall, his arms
hanging by his sides, and his face as white as
paper. He had just received a bullet in the
breast, but the old man's warrior soul was still
strong within him, as he cried:

"Defend yourselves, conscripts! Defend yourselves! Show the Kaiserliks that a French soldier is yet worth four of them! ah the vil-
lains!"

We heard the sound of blows on the door
below thundering like cannon-shot. We still kept
up our fire, but hopelessly, when we heard the
clatter of hoofs without. The firing ceased, and
we saw through the smoke four squadrons of
lancers dashing like a troop of lions through the
midst of the Austrians. All yielded before them.
The Kaiserliks fled, but the long, blue lances

with their red pennons, were swifter than they, and many a white coat was pierced from behind. The lancers were Poles—the most terrible warriors I have ever seen, and, to speak truth, our friends, and our brothers. *They* never turned from us in our hour of need; they gave us the last drop of their blood. And what have we done for their unhappy country? When I think of our ingratitude, my heart bleeds.

The Poles rescued us. Seeing them so proud and brave, we rushed out, attacking the Austrians with the bayonet, and driving them into the trenches. We were for the time victorious, but it was time to beat a retreat, for the enemy were already filling Leipzig; the gates of Halle and Grimma were orced, and that of Peters-Thau delivered up by our friends the Badeners and our other friends the Saxons. Soldiers, citizens, and students kept up a fire from the windows on our retiring troops.

We had only time to re-form and take the road along the Pleisse; the lancers awaited us there: we defiled behind them, and, as the Austrians again pressed around us, they charged once more to drive them back. What brave fellows and magnificent horsemen were those Poles!

How those who saw them charge—in such a moment—must admire them!

The division, reduced from fifteen to eight thousand men, retired step by step before fifty thousand foes, and not without often turning and replying to the Austrian fire.

We neared the bridge—with what joy, I need not say. But it was no easy task to reach it, for infantry and horse crowded the whole width of the avenue, and continued to come from all the neighboring roads, until the crowd formed an impenetrable mass, which advanced slowly, with groans and smothered cries, which might be heard at a distance of half a mile, despite the rattling of musketry. Woe to those upon the sides of the bridge! they were forced into the water and no one stretched a hand to save them. In the middle, men and even horses were carried along with the crowd; they had no need of making any exertion of their own. But how were we to get there? The enemy were advancing nearer and nearer every moment. It is true we had stationed a few cannon so as to sweep the principal approaches, and some troops yet remained in line to repulse their attacks; but they had guns to sweep the bridge, and those who remained behind must receive their whole fire. This accounted for the press on the bridge.

At two or three hundred paces from the bridge, the idea of rushing forward and throwing myself into the midst of the crowd, entered my mind; but Captain Vidal, Lieutenant Brétonville, and other old officers said :

"Shoot down the first man that leaves the ranks!"

It was horrible to be so near safety, and yet unable to escape.

This was between eleven and twelve o'clock. The fusilade grew nearer on the right and left, and a few bullets began to whistle over our heads. From the side of Halle we saw the Prussians rush pell-mell out with our own soldiers. Terrible cries now arose from the bridge. Cavalry, to make way for themselves, sabred the infantry, who replied with the bayonet. It was a general *sauve qui peut*. At every movement of the crowd, some one fell from the bridge, and, trying to regain his place, dragged five or six with him into the water.

In the midst of this horrible confusion, this pandemonium of shouts, cries, groans, musket-shots, and sabre-strokes, a crash like a peal of thunder was heard, and the first arch of the bridge rose upward into the air with all upon it. Hundreds of wretches were torn to pieces, and hundreds of others were crushed beneath the falling ruins.

A sapper had blown up the arch!

At this sight, the cry of treason rang from mouth to mouth. "We are lost—betrayed!" was now the cry on all sides. The tumult was fearful. Some, in the rage of despair, turned upon the enemy like wild beasts at bay, thinking only of vengeance; others broke their arms, cursing heaven and earth for their misfortunes. Mounted officers and generals dashed into the river to cross it by swimming, and many soldiers followed them without taking time to throw off their knapsacks. The thought that the last hope of safety was gone, and nothing now remained but to be massacred, made men mad. I had seen the Partha choked with dead bodies the day before, but this scene was a thousand times more horrible; drowning wretches dragging down those who happened to be near them; shrieks and yells of rage, or for help; a broad river concealed by a mass of heads and struggling arms.

Captain Vidal, who, by his coolness and steady

eye, had hitherto kept us to our duty, even Captain Vidal now appeared discouraged. He thrust his sabre into the scabbard, and cried, with a strange laugh:

"The game is up! Let us be gone!"

I touched his arm; he looked sadly and kindly at me.

"What do you wish, my child?" he asked.

"Captain," said I, "I was four months in the hospital at Leipzig: I have bathed in the Elster, and I know a ford."

"Where?"

"Ten minutes' march above the bridge."

He drew his sabre at once from its sheath, and shouted:

"Follow me, my boys, and you, Bertha, lead."

The entire battalion, which did not now number more than two hundred men, followed; a hundred others, who saw us start confidently forward, joined us without knowing where we were going. The Austrians were already on the terrace of the avenue; further down, gardens, separated by hedges, stretched to the Elster. I recognized the road which Zimmer and I had traversed so often in July, when the ground was covered with flowers. The enemy fired on us, but we did not reply. I entered the water first; Captain Vidal next, then the others, two abreast. It reached our shoulders, for the river was swollen by the autumn rains; but we crossed, notwithstanding, without the loss of a man. Nearly all of us had our muskets when we reached the other bank, and we pressed onward across the fields, and soon reached the little wooden bridge at Schleissig, and thence turned to Lindenau.

We marched silently, turning from time to time to gaze on the other side of the Elster, where the battle still raged in the streets of Leipzig. The furious shouts, and the deep boom of cannon still reached our ears; and it was only when, about two o'clock, we overtook the long column which stretched, till lost in the distance, on the road to Erfurt, that the sounds of conflict were lost in the roll of wagons and artillery trains.

XXI.

HITHERTO I have described the grandeur of war —battles glorious to France, notwithstanding our mistakes and misfortunes. When we were fighting all Europe alone, always one against two, and often one to three; when we finally succumbed, not through the courage of our foes, but borne down by treason, and the weight of numbers, we had no reason to blush for our defeat, and the victors have little reason to exult in it. It is not numbers that makes the glory of a people or an army—it is virtue and bravery. This is what I think in all sincerity, and I believe that right feeling, sensible men in every country will think the same.

But now I must relate the horrors of retreat, and this is the hardest part of my task. It is said that confidence gives strength, and this is especially true of the French. While they advanced in full hope of victory, they were united; the will of their chiefs was their only law; they knew that they could succeed only by strict observance of discipline. But when driven back, no one had confidence save in himself, and commands were forgotten. Then these men—once so brave and so proud, who marched so gayly to the fight—scattered to right and left; sometimes fleeing alone, sometimes in groups. Then those who, a little while before, trembled at their approach, grew bold; they came on, first timidly, but, meeting no resistance, became insolent. Then they would swoop down and carry off three or four laggards at a time, as I have seen crows in winter swoop upon a fallen horse, which they did not dare approach while he could yet remain on his feet.

I have seen miserable Cossacks—very beggars, with nothing but old rags hanging around them; an old cap of tattered skin over their ears; unshorn beards, covered with vermin; mounted on old worn-out horses, without saddles, and with only a piece of rope by way of stirrups, an old rusty pistol all their fire-arms, and a nail at the end of a pole for a lance; I have seen those wretches, who resembled sallow and decrepit Jews more than soldiers, stop ten, fifteen, twenty of our men, and lead them off like sheep.

And the tall, lank peasants, who, a few months before, trembled if we only looked at them—I have seen them arrogantly repulse old soldiers—cuirassiers, artillerymen, dragoons who had fought through the Spanish war, men who could have crushed them with a blow of their fist; I have seen these peasants insist that they had no bread to sell, while the odor of the oven arose on all sides of us; that they had no wine, no beer, when we heard glasses clinking to right and left. And no one dared punish them; no one dared take what he wanted from the wretches who laughed to see us in such straits, for each one was retreating on his own account; we had no leaders, no discipline, and they could easily out-number us.

And to hunger, misery, weariness, and fever, the horrors of an approaching winter were added. The rain never ceased falling from the gray sky, and the winds pierced us to the bones. How could poor beardless conscripts, mere shadows, fleshless and worn out, endure all this? They perished by thousands; their bodies covered the roads. The terrible *typhus* pursued us. Some said it was a plague, engendered by the dead not being buried deep enough; others, that it was the consequence of sufferings that required more than human strength to bear. I know not how this may be, but the villages of Alsace and Lorraine, to which we brought it, will long remember their sufferings; of a hundred attacked by it, not more than ten or twelve, at the most, recovered.

At length—since I must continue this sad story—on the evening of the nineteenth, we bivouacked at Lutzen, where our regiments re-formed as best they might. The next day early, as we marched on Weissenfels, we had to skirmish with the Westphalians, who followed us as far as the village of Eglaystadt. The twenty-second we bivouacked on the glacis at Erfurt, where we received new shoes and uniforms. Five or six disbanded companies joined our battalion—nearly all conscripts. Our new coats and shoes were much too large for us; but they were warm; we felt like new men.

We had to start again the twenty-second, and the following days passed near Götha, Teitlebe,

Eisenach and Salminster. The Cossacks reconnoitred us from a distance. Our hussars would drive them off; but they returned the moment pursuit was relaxed. Many of our men went pillaging in the night, and were absent at roll-call, and the sentries received orders to shoot all who attempted to leave their bivouacs.

I had had the fever ever since we left Leipzig; it increased day by day, and I became so weak that I could scarcely rise in the mornings to follow the march. Zébédé looked sadly at me, and sometimes said:

"Courage, Joseph! We will soon be at home!"

These words reanimated me; I felt my face flush.

"Yes, yes!" I said; "we will soon be home; I must see home once more!"

The tears forced themselves to my eyes. Zébédé carried my knapsack when I was tired, and continued:

"Lean on my arm. We are getting nearer every day, now, Joseph. A few dozen leagues are nothing."

My heart beat more bravely, but my strength was gone. I could no longer carry my musket; it was heavy as lead. I could not eat; my knees trembled beneath me; still I did not despair, but kept murmuring to myself: "this is nothing. When you see the clock-tower of Phalsbourg, your fever will leave you. You will have good air, and Catharine will nurse you. All will yet be well!"

Others, no worse than I, fell by the roadside, but still I toiled on; when near Folde, we learned that fifty thousand Bavarians were posted in the forests through which we were to pass, for the purpose of cutting off our retreat. This was my finishing stroke, for I knew I could no longer load, fire, or defend myself with the bayonet. I felt that all my sufferings to get so far toward home were useless. Nevertheless, I made an effort, when we were ordered to march, and tried to rise.

"Come, come, Joseph!" said Zébédé; "courage!"

But I could not move, and lay sobbing like a child.

"Come, stand up!" he said.

"I cannot. O God! I cannot!"

I clutched his arm. Tears streamed down his face. He tried to lift me, but he was too weak. I held fast to him, crying:

"Zébédé, do not abandon me!"

Captain Vidal approached, and gazed sadly on me.

"Cheer up, my lad," said he; "the ambulances will be along in half an hour."

But I knew what that meant, and I drew Zébédé closer to me. He embraced me, and I whispered in his ear:

"Kiss Catharine for me—promise! Tell her that I died thinking of her, and bear her my last farewell!"

"Yes, yes!" he sobbed. "My poor Joseph!"

I could cling to him no longer. He placed me on the ground, and ran away without turning his head. The column departed, and I gazed at it as one who sees his last hope fading from his eyes. The last of the battalion disappeared over the ridge of a hill. I closed my eyes. An hour passed, or perhaps a longer time, when the boom of cannon startled me, and I saw a division of the guard pass at a quick step with artillery and wagons. Seeing some sick in the wagons, I cried, wistfully:

"Take me! Take me!"

But no one listened; still they kept on, while the thunder of artillery grew louder and louder.

More than ten thousand men, cavalry and infantry, passed me, but I had no longer strength to call out to them.

At last the long line ended; I saw knapsacks and shakos disappear behind the hill, and I lay down to sleep for ever, when once more I was aroused by the rolling of five or six pieces of artillery along the road. The cannoneers sat sabre in hand, and behind came the caissons. I hoped no more from these than from the others, when suddenly I perceived a tall, lean, red-bearded veteran mounted beside one of the pieces, and bearing the cross upon his breast. It was my old friend Zimmer, my old comrade of Leipzig. He was passing without seeing me, when I cried, with all the strength that remained to me:

"Christian! Christian!"

He heard me in spite of the noise of the guns; stopped, and turned round.

"Christian!" I cried, "take pity on me!"

He saw me lying at the foot of a tree, and came to me with a pale face and staring eyes:

"What! Is it you, my poor Joseph?" cried he, springing from his horse.

He lifted me in his arms as if I were an infant, and shouted to the men who were driving the last wagon:

"Halt!"

Then embracing me, he placed me in it, my head upon a knapsack. I saw too that he wrapped a great cavalry cloak around my feet, as he cried:

"Forward! Forward! It is growing warm yonder!"

I remember no more, but I have the faint impression of hearing the sound of heavy guns and rattle of musketry, mingled with shouts and commands. Branches of tall pines seemed to pass between me and the sky through the night; but all this might have been a dream. But that day, behind Solmunster, in the woods of Hanau, we had a battle with the Bavarians, and routed them.

XXII.

ON the fifteenth of January, 1814, two months and a half after the battle of Hanau, I awoke in a good bed, and at the end of a little, well-warmed room; and gazing at the rafters over my head, then at the little windows, where the frost had spread its silver sheen, I exclaimed: "It is winter!" At the same time I heard the crash of artillery and the crackling of a fire, and turning over on my bed in a few moments, I saw seated at its side a pale young woman, with her arms folded, and I recognized—Catharine! I recognized, too, the room where I had spent so many happy Sundays before going to the wars. But the thunder of the cannon made me think I was dreaming. I gazed for a long while at Catharine, who seemed more beautiful than ever, and the question rose, "Where is Aunt

I AWOKE IN A GOOD BED. (Page 324.)

Gredel? am I at home once more? God grant that this be not a dream!"

At last I took courage and called softly:

"Catharine!" And she, turning her head cried: "Joseph! Do you know me?"

"Yes," I replied, holding out my hand.

She approached, trembling and sobbing, when again and again the cannon thundered.

"What are those shots I hear?" I cried.

"The guns of Phalsbourg," she answered. "The city is besieged."

"Phalsbourg besieged! The enemy in France!"

I could speak no more. Thus had so much suffering, so many tears, so many thousands of lives gone for nothing, ay, worse than nothing, for the foe was at our homes. For an hour I could think of nothing else; and now, old and gray-haired as I am, the thought fills me with bitterness. Yes, we old men have seen the German, the Russian, the Swede, the Spaniard, the Englishman, masters of France, garrisoning our cities, taking whatever suited them from our fortesses, insulting our soldiers, changing our flag, and dividing among themselves, not only our conquests since 1804, but even those of the Republic. These were the fruits of ten years of glory!

But let us not speak of these things, the future will pass upon them. They will tell us that after Lutzen and Bautzen, the enemy offered to leave us Belgium, part of Holland, all the left bank of the Rhine as far as Bâle, with Savoy and the kingdom of Italy; and that the Emperor refused to accept these conditions, brilliant as they were, because he placed the satisfaction of his own pride before the happiness of France!

But to return to my story. For two weeks after the battle of Hanau, thousands of wagons, filled with wounded, crowded the road from Strasbourg to Nancy, and passed through Phalsbourg.

They stretched in one long line through all Alsace to Lorraine.

Not one in the sad *cortége* escaped the eyes of Aunt Grédel and Catharine. What their thoughts were, I need not say. More than twelve hundred wagons had passed;—I was in none of them. Thousands of fathers and mothers sought among them for their children. How many returned without them!

The third day Catharine found me among a heap of other wretches, in basket wagons from Mayence, with sunken cheeks and glaring eyes—

dying of hunger. She knew me at once, but Aunt Grédel gazed long before she cried: '

"Yes! it is he! It is Joseph!"

She took me home, and watched over me night and day. I wanted only water, for which I constantly shrieked. No one in the village believed that I would ever recover, but the happiness of breathing my native air and of once more seeing those I loved, saved me.

It was about six months after, on the 15th of July, 1814, that Catharine and I were married; Monsieur Goulden, who loved us as his own children, gave me half his business, and we lived together as happy as birds.

Then the wars were ended; the allies gradually returned to their homes; the Emperor went to Elba, and King Louis XVIII. gave us a reasonable amount of liberty. Once more the sweet days of youth returned—the days of love, of labor, and of peace. The future was once more full of hope—of hope that every one, by good conduct and economy, would at some time attain a position in the world, win the esteem of good men, and raise his family without fear of being carried off by the conscription seven or eiglt years after.

Monsieur Goulden, who was not too well satisfied at seeing the old kings and nobility return, thought, notwithstanding, that they had suffered enough in foreign lands to understand that they were not the only people in the world, and to respect our rights; he thought, too, that the Emperor Napoleon would have the good sense to remain quiet—but he was mistaken. The Bourbons returned with their old notions, and the Emperor only awaited the moment of vengeance.

All this was to bring more miseries upon us, which I would willingly relate, if this story did not seem already long enough. But here let us rest. If people of sense tell me that I have done well in relating my campaign of 1813—that my story may show youth the vanity of military glory, and prove that no man can gain happiness save by peace, liberty, and labor—then I will take up my pen once more, and give you the story of Waterloo!

THE END.

BY

THE CONSCRIPT,

A Tale of the French War of 1813.

By MM. ERCKMANN-CHATRIAN.

With Eight Full-Page Illustrations.

One Vol. 12mo.   **Price $1.50.**

FROM THE LONDON ARMY AND NAVY GAZETTE.

"Since the days of De Foe, there was probably never written a fiction which looked so like truth as this of the great Napoleonic wars. Indeed, it can hardly be called a fiction, except in the names which are given to the characters, for the incidents will all bear the test of historical comparison, and the *dramatis personæ* are perfect types of the good people of the Alsatian border, of which the Conscript is a native. . . . . He gives a true and most touching account of the miseries of war, and his description of the battle of Leipzig might be taken as a model by our military historians."

ALSO, JUST PUBLISHED,

MADAME THÉRÈSE;

Or, The Volunteers of '92.

By MM. ERCKMANN-CHATRIAN.

With Ten Full-page Illustrations.

One Vol. 12mo.   **Price $1.50.**

MADAME THERESE; OR, THE VOLUNTEERS OF 1792, is the story of a *vivandière* in the army of the Moselle,—a division of the Republican forces,—left for dead on the battle-field of Anstatt, rescued and brought back to life by a brave German doctor. The story abounds in graphic pictures of country life on the borders of France, and is one of the most charming of modern fictitious productions.

WATERLOO.

A Sequel to the Conscript of 1813.

By ERCKMANN-CHATRIAN.

One vol., 12mo, uniform with "Madame Therese" and the "Conscript."

With Six Full-Page Illustrations.   *Price $1.50.*

In Waterloo, Joseph continues the story so charmingly begun in the Conscript. The description of the battle of Waterloo, coming, as it pretends to do, from a soldier actually engaged in the great struggle, is one of the most vivid and graphic ever written.

CRITICAL NOTICE.

"We have never read a more graphic description than our author gives of those successive stages of agony through which the Conscripts and their families had to pass. . . . All this, and much more, is sketched with a few bold strokes, tempered with charming humor."—*London Times.*

MADAME THERESE,

Or, the Volunteers of '92. By MM. Erckmann-Chatrian. With ten full-page illustrations. One vol. 12mo. Price $1.50.

The story is full of graphic and minute descriptions turning a good deal on the Duke of Brunswick's march, Hoche and the military movements, and the rights of man. The simple manner of the boy-narrator gives it a vivid air of reality, well sustained by the translation of Miss Charlotte Forten, which does not read at all like a translation, but runs in an easy and animated style. The book has ten full-page illustrations, executed in a very expressive and peculiarly French manner.—*N. Y. Times.*

These writers are absolutely unequalled in their own peculiar field. The simple, faithful realism of their style only brings out into stronger relief the noble purpose which animates all the works of which "Madame Therese" is one. False glory, military ambition, and war never perhaps had enemies more powerful appearing in so modest a form.—*New York Independent.*

As a story it is full of interest of the most legitimate kind; as a picture of a period when the great deeps were broken up, it is masterly; and as a study of character, it is worthy of George Sand.—*New York Albion.*

The story is a picturesque one, and the pictures are drawn with a pre-Raphaelite minuteness and fidelity, and describe French country life in a way made peculiarly interesting by a constant vivacity of imagination and of style.—*Boston Congregationalist.*

It is characterized by a beautiful simplicity which never becomes low or silly. One who begins it is not likely to leave off before finishing. And it wears throughout the impress of truth to life and nature.—*New York Examiner.*

It contains a fine and faithful picture of French rural life, given with great simplicity, and the book is evidently immeasurably above the miserable, immoral French novels, which are so abundant and so nasty.—*Philadelphia Presbyterian.*

The romances of these friendly writers occupy a place in fiction similar to that which the pictures of Frère or Meyer Von Bremen occupy in art.—*N. Y. Evening Post.*

More interesting than anything by Miss Muhlbach.—*Lutheran Observer (Philadelphia).*

A story, and a good one, of the French battle-days of '92, full of huge grenadiers, citizeness "cantinières," war, onslaught, and so on. Written with dash and fire, and worth having.—*New York World.*

It is a boy's story—that is, supposed to be written by a boy,—and has all the freshness, the unconscious simplicity and *naïveté* which the imagined authorship should imply; while nothing more graphic, more clearly and vividly pictorial, has been brought before the public for many a day.—*Boston Commonwealth.*

THE CONSCRIPT.

By MM. Erckmann-Chatrian. With eight full-page illustrations. One vol. 12mo. Price $1.50.

"We have never read a more graphic description than our author gives of those successive stages of agony through which the Conscripts and their families had to pass. . . . . All this, and much more, is sketched with a few bold strokes, tempered with charming humor."—*London Times.*

"It reads very much like a real story, and it is told with a quaint simplicity and truthfulness which will win the reader's heart."—*London Athenæum.*

"A series of fascinating sketches of love and war. . . . There is an air of reality about these sketches which makes them read like veritable autobiography, and that of a very interesting kind. The characters are numerous for a short story, sufficiently defined, and agreeable."—*The London Illustrated Times.*

CONSTANCE AYLMER.

A Story of the Seventeenth Century. One vol. 12mo. Price $1.50.

"It is quite equal in ability to several volumes of the Schonberg-Cotta Series, and does a sort of justice to Old England, and old New England, and early Dutch life, which it is pleasant to see. Without a taint of sensationalism, it is a thoroughly interesting book, and cannot fail to do good."—*Boston Congregationalist.*

"The style is pure and simple, and the story one of real interest."—*Philadelphia Presbyterian.*

"The story has no feverish excitement about it, but in its stead will please by its general fidelity to the manners and spirit of the period in which its scenes are laid."—*Cincinnati Gazette.*

"There is interest enough in the tale itself and glimpses of old Colonial life, both authentic and artistic, to make the little romance entertaining and suggestive—more so than many of the popular fictions of more ambitious aim and less local significance."—*Boston Transcript.*

"A vivid picture of bygone people and times."—*Philadelphia Inquirer.*

"In many respects one of the finest books of the kind we ever read."—*Chicago Journal.*

CHARLES SCRIBNER.   A. C. ARMSTRONG.
          A. J. PEABODY.   EDWARD SEYMOUR.

Condensed Catalogue

OF THE PUBLICATIONS OF

CHARLES SCRIBNER & Co.,

654 BROADWAY,

NEW YORK.

*** *The figures in the last column of this Catalogue refer to* CHARLES SCRIBNER & CO.'S *Descriptive Catalogue, copies of which will be sent to any address upon application.*

*** *Blanks in the column of prices, except in the case of School Text-Books, the prices of which may be learned from* CHARLES SCRIBNER & CO.'S *Educational Catalogue, indicate that the Works are either out of print or in press.*

*** *In this list the names of Books just published are given in* SMALL CAPITALS; *those issued during the year* 1868, *as well as new editions of Works previously produced, are indicated by italics.*

*** *The prices here given are for the regular style of binding in cloth. Books furnished in other styles, and their respective prices, may be learned from the Descriptive Catalogue.*

*** *Any of these Books will be sent post-paid to any address upon receipt of the price.*

	Volumes.	Size.	Price.	Page.
ADAMS, W., D.D.				
Thanksgiving	1	12mo	$2 00	2
Three Gardens	1	12mo	2 00	1
AGASSIZ, PROF. LOUIS.				
Structure of Animal Life (The) . .	1	8vo	2 50	2
ALEXANDER, A., D.D.				
Moral Science	1	12mo	1 50	3
ALEXANDER, REV. H. C.				
LIFE OF J. ADDISON ALEXANDER . .	2	cr. 8vo	5 00	9
ALEXANDER, J. W., D.D.				
Alexander, Archibald, Life of (Portrait) .	1	12mo	2 25	3
Christian Faith and Practice (Discourses) .	1	12mo	2 00	6
Consolation (Discourses)	1	12mo	2 00	5
Faith (Discourses)	1	12mo	2 00	6
Forty Years' Correspondence with a Friend	1	12mo	2 50	4
Preaching, Thoughts on	1	12mo	2 00	5

	Volumes.	Size.	Price.	Page.
ALEXANDER, J. A., D.D.				
Acts (Commentary)	2	12mo	$4 00	8
Isaiah " (complete)	2	8vo	6 50	7
" " (abridged)	2	12mo	4 00	8
Mark "	1	12mo	2 00	8
Matthew "	1	12mo	2 00	8
Psalms "	2	12mo	5 00	7
New Test. Literature and Ecc. History	1	12mo	2 00	9
Sermons (with Portrait)	1	12mo	2 50	9
ALLSTON, WASHINGTON.				
Lectures and Poems	1	12mo	2 50	10
ANDERSON, R., D.D.				
Foreign Missions	1	12mo	1 50	10
ANDREWS, REV. S. J.				
Life of Our Lord	1	post 8vo	3 00	11
ARMSTRONG, G. D., D.D.				
Works of	3	12mo ea.	1 25	12
BAUTAIN, PROF. A.				
Extempore Speaking	1	12mo	1 50	13
BEECHER, REV. H. W.				
Prayers from Plymouth Pulpit	1	12mo	1 75	14
Norwood	1	12mo	1 50	14
BOTTA, PROF.				
Dante as Poet, Patriot, Philosopher	1	crown 8vo	2 50	15
BRACE, CHARLES L.				
Hungary, with Experience of Austrian Police	1	12mo	—	16
Home Life in Germany	1	12mo	—	15
Norse Folk	1	12mo	2 00	16
Races of Old World	1	post 8vo	2 50	16
Short Sermons for Newsboys	1	16mo	1 50	17
BUSHNELL, HORACE, D.D.				
Character of Jesus	1	18mo	1 00	20
Christ and his Salvation	1	12mo	2 00	20
Christian Nurture	1	12mo	2 00	19
Moral Uses of Dark Things	1	12mo	2 00	21
Nature and the Supernatural	1	12mo	2 25	18
New Life, Sermons for	1	12mo	2 00	20
Vicarious Sacrifice, The	1	12mo	2 25	19
Women's Suffrage	1	12mo	1 50	21
Work and Play	1	12mo	2 00	20
CHEEVER, G. B., D.D. Works of	3	12mo	—	22
CLARK, PROF. N. G.				
English Language, Elements of	1	12mo	1 25	23

	Volumes.	Size.	Price.	Page.
COLLIER, J. PAYNE, F.S.A.				
Rarest Books in English Language	4	cr. 8vo	$12 00	23
CONYBEARE, REV. W. J., and HOWSON, REV. J. S.				
St Paul, Life and Epistles of (illustrated)	1	8vo	3 00	24
CONSTANCE AYLMER	1	12mo	1 50	28
COOK, PROF. J. P., JR.				
Religion and Chemistry	1	cr. 8vo	2 50	26
COOLEY, PROF. LE ROY.				
NATURAL PHILOSOPHY	1	12mo	1 50	27
CHEMISTRY	1	12mo	1 25	28
CRAIK, GEO. L., LL.D.				
English Literature and Language	2	8vo	7 50	25
CROSBY, PROF. HOWARD, D.D.				
New Testament with Notes	1	12mo	1 50	26
CRUMMELL, REV. A.				
Africa, Future of	1	12mo	1 00	—
DALGLEISH, W. S.				
GRAMMATICAL ANALYSIS	1	12mo	75	29
DANA, A. H.				
Ethical and Physiological Inquiries	1	12mo	1 50	30
DANA, R. H.				
Poems and Prose Writings	2	12mo	4 00	30
DAWSON, HENRY B.				
Fœderalist, with Notes	1	8vo	3 75	30
DAY, PROF. H. N.				
AMERICAN SPELLER	1	16mo	25	33
English Composition	1	12mo	1 50	31
Discourse (Rhetoric)	1	12mo	1 50	31
ENGLISH LITERATURE	1	12mo	2 25	33
Logic	1	12mo	1 50	32
DERBY, EDWARD, EARL OF.				
Homer's Iliad (translated)	2	cr. 8vo	5 00	34
DE VERE, M. SCHELE, LL.D.				
Studies in English	1	cr. 8vo	2 50	35
DINGMAN, J. H.				
Publisher's Sheet-Book	1	Folio	15 00	35
DIVINE TEACHER	1	16mo	1 50	38
DRUMMOND, REV. JAS.				
Christian Life, Thoughts for	1	12mo	1 50	36

	Volumes.	Size.	Price.	Page.
DUYCKINCK, E. A. and G. L.				
Cyclopædia of Am. Literature (400 Portraits, &c.)	2	royal 8vo	$10 00	37
DWIGHT, BENJ. W.				
Philology, Modern	2	8vo	6 00	36
ELLET, MRS. E. F.				
American Revolution, Domestic History of	1	12mo	1 50	38
" " Women of	3	12mo	——	39
Pioneer Women of the West	1	12mo	1 50	38
Queens of Am. Society (14 steel engravings)	1	12mo	3 00	39
ELLIOTT, CHARLES W.				
New England History	2	8vo	6 00	40
ERCKMANN-CHATRIAN.				
MADAME THERESE	1	12mo	1 50	41
CONSCRIPT	1	12mo	1 50	41
WATERLOO	1	12mo	1 50	41
EWBANK, THOS.				
Hydraulics	1	8vo	6 00	40
FELTER, S. A.				
Arithmetics, Natural Series of	1	——	——	42–43
FIELD, HENRY M., D.D.				
Atlantic Telegraph, History of	1	12mo	1 75	44
FISHER, REV. PROF. GEO. P.				
Supernatural Origin of Christianity	1	8vo	3 00	45
Silliman, Benj., LL. D., Life of (Portrait)	2	cr. 8vo	5 00	44
FORSYTH, WM.				
Cicero, New Life of (Illustrations)	2	cr. 8vo	5 00	46
FOWLER, W. C., LL.D.				
Sectional Controversy (The)	1	8vo	2 00	46
FROUDE, J. A.				
HISTORY OF ENGLAND	12	cr. 8vo	3 00 ea.	47
SHORT STUDIES ON GREAT SUBJECTS	1	cr. 8vo	3 00	48
GAGE, REV. W. L.				
Carl Ritter, Life of	1	12mo	2 00	49
GASPARIN, COUNT.				
America before Europe	1	12mo	2 00	49
GIBBONS, J. S.				
Public Debt of the United States	1	cr. 8vo	2 00	50
GUIZOT, M.				
Meditations (First and Second Series)	2	12mo ea.	1 75	50

		Volumes.	Size.	Price.	Page.
GUYOT, PROF. ARNOLD.					
Geographies, Wall Maps, Key, etc.		—	—	—	51–54
HALL, EDWIN, D.D.					
Puritans and their Principles		1	8vo	$2 50	55
HALSEY, REV. LEROY J.					
Bible, Literary Attractions of		1	12mo	1 75	55
HAMILTON, J. A.					
REMINISCENCES		1	8vo	5 00	56
HARPER, MRS. M. J.					
PRACTICAL COMPOSITION		1	12mo	90	56
HEADLEY, J. T.					
Complete Works of		15			57–61
HEIDELBERG,					
Catechism		1	small 4to	3 50	62
HERBERT, H. W.					
Works of		3	12mo ea.	1 50	62
HOLLAND, DR. J. G. (Timothy Titcomb).					
Bay-Path. A Novel		1	12mo	2 00	66
Bitter-Sweet. A Poem		1	12mo	1 50	64
Gold Foil		1	12mo	1 75	64
Kathrina. A Poem		1	12mo	1 50	67
Lessons in Life		1	12mo	1 75	65
Letters to the Joneses		1	12mo	1 75	65
Letters to Young People		1	12mo	1 50	63
Miss Gilbert's Career		1	12mo	2 00	67
Plain Talks on Familiar Subjects		1	12mo	1 75	66
HOPKINS, MARK, D.D.					
LAW OF LOVE		1	12mo	1 75	68
HOURS AT HOME.					
A FAMILY MAGAZINE		Per annum		3 00	69
HURST, REV. J. F.					
HAGENBACH'S CHURCH HISTORY		2	8vo	6 00	71
Rationalism, History of		1	8vo	3 50	70
ILLUSTRATED LIBRARY OF WONDERS.					
WONDERS OF OPTICS		1	12mo	1 50	72
WONDERS OF HEAT		1	12mo	1 50	74
THUNDER AND LIGHTNING		1	12mo	1 50	73
INTELLIGENCE OF ANIMALS		1	12mo	1 50	74
GREAT HUNTS		1	12mo	1 50	75
EGYPT 3300 YEARS AGO		1	12mo	1 50	75
WONDERS OF POMPEII		1	12mo	1 50	75
THE SUBLIME IN NATURE		1	12mo	1 50	75

	Volumes.	Size.	Price.	Page.
THE SUN	1	12mo	$1 50	75
WONDERS OF ITALIAN ART	1	12mo	1 50	75
WONDERS OF GLASS MAKING,	1	12mo	1 50	75
BOTTOM OF THE OCEAN (*In Press*)	1	12mo	1 50	75
WONDERS OF ARCHITECTURE (*In Press*)	1	12mo	1 50	75
ACOUSTICS (*In Press*)	1	12mo	1 50	75
THE HUMAN FRAME (*In Press*)	1	12mo	1 50	75

JAMESON, JUDGE J. A.
Constitutional Convention	1	8vo	4 50	71

JENNINGS, L. J.
Republican Government in the U. S.	1	12mo	1 75	76

JOHNSON, ANNA C. (Minnie Myrtle).
Cottages of the Alps	1	12mo	——	76
Germany, Peasant Life in	1	12mo	——	76
Myrtle Wreath	1	12mo	1 25	76

JONES, CHARLES COLCOCK, D.D.
HISTORY OF THE CHURCH OF GOD	2	8vo ea.	3 50	76

KIRKLAND, MRS. C. M.
Evening Book	1	12mo	1 25	78
Holidays Abroad	2	12mo	2 00	78
Patriotic Eloquence	1	12mo	1 75	77
School Garland	1	12mo	——	77

KNOX, J. B.
History of West Indies	1	12mo	1 50	78

LABOULAYE, EDOUARD.
Paris in America	1	12mo	1 25	83

LANGE, PROF. J. P., D.D.
Commentary on Scriptures, Theolog. and Homiletical: *Genesis* (1); Matthew (1); *Mark and Luke* (1); *Acts* (1); ROMANS (1); *James, Peter, John, Jude* (1); *Corinthians* (1); *Thessalonians, Timothy, Titus, Philemon, Hebrews* (1); PROVERBS (1); Ecclesiastes, SONG OF SOLOMON (1)		8vo ea.	5 00	79–82

LAWRENCE, EUGENE.
British Historians, Lives of	2	12mo	3 50	83

LIBER LIBRORUM	1	16mo	1 50	84

LILLIE, JOHN, D.D.
LECTURES ON THE EPISTLES OF PETER	1	8vo	3 50	84

LORD, JOHN, LL.D.
Old Roman World	1	cr. 8vo	3 00	85
ANCIENT STATES AND EMPIRES	1	cr. 8vo	3 00	85

www.ingramcontent.com/pod-product-compliance
Lightning Source LLC
Chambersburg PA
CBHW021152230426
43667CB00006B/357